History Makers

Louis Armstrong

Jazz Musician

Joel Newsome

New York

Published in 2018 by Cavendish Square Publishing, LLC
243 5th Avenue, Suite 136, New York, NY 10016

First Edition

Library of Congress Cataloging-in-Publication Data

Names: Newsome, Joel, 1984- author.
Title: Louis Armstrong : jazz musician / Joel Newsome.
Description: New York : Cavendish Square Publishing, [2018] I
Series: History makers I Includes bibliographical references and index.
Identifiers: LCCN 2017021455 (print) I LCCN 2017021952 (ebook) I
ISBN 9781502633217 (E-book) I ISBN 9781502632920 (library bound)
Subjects: LCSH: Armstrong, Louis, 1901-1971--Juvenile literature. I
Jazz musicians--United States--Biography--Juvenile literature.
Classification: LCC ML3930.A75 (ebook) I LCC ML3930.A75 N49 2018 (print) I
DDC 781.65092 [B] --dc23
LC record available at https://lccn.loc.gov/2017021455

Editorial Director: David McNamara
Editor: Kristen Susienka
Copy Editor: Rebecca Rohan
Associate Art Director: Amy Greenan
Designer: Jessica Nevins
Production Coordinator: Karol Szymczuk
Photo Research: J8 Media

The photographs in this book are used by permission and through the courtesy of: Cover FPG/Archive Photos/Getty Images; p. 4 Bettmann/Getty Images; p. 8 Amadeustx/Shutterstock.com; p. 11 Pictorial Press Ltd/Alamy; p. 13 Susan Wood/Getty Images/Archive Photos/Getty Images; p. 16 Apic/Hulton Archive/Getty Images; pp. 23, 40, 105 Pictorial Press Ltd/Alamy; pp. 26, 30 GAB Archive/Redferns/Getty Images; p. 36 Heritage Image Partnership Ltd/Alamy; p. 42 Gilles Petard/Redferns/Getty Images; p. 48 Bridgeman Images; p. 51 Chicago History Museum/Archive Photos/Getty Images; p. 56 PhotoQuest/Archive Photos/Getty Images; p. 61 Sheridan Libraries/Levy/Gado/Archive Photos/Getty Images; pp. 64, 77, 113 Michael Ochs Archives/Getty Images; p. 71 Charles Peterson/Hulton Archive/Getty Images; p. 72 John Loengard/The LIFE Picture Collection/Getty Images; pp. 82, 125 ©AP Images; p. 86 Photo 12/Universal Images Group/Getty Images; p. 91 Mondadori Portfolio/Getty Images; p. 100 John D. Kisch/Separate Cinema Archive/Moviepix/Getty Images; p. 116 Leo Vals/Archive Photos/Getty Images; p. 121 Afro Newspaper/Gado/Archive Photos/Getty Images; p. 129 David Redfern/Redferns/Getty Images.

Printed in the United States of America

Table of Contents

ong's Hot Five,
keh Record Artists.

1 From a Boy in "The Battlefield" to the Top of the Charts

"The bottom line of any country in the world is 'what did we contribute to the world?' ... We contributed Louis Armstrong."

Tony Bennett
New York Times, 1944

Before hip-hop and rock 'n' roll, jazz was king. It completely changed music and was the first truly American art form. Improvisation, 4/4 time, the solo—all of these came from jazz, and Louis Armstrong perfected the art form.

Jazz was originally a combination of the blues, soulful music that had evolved from spirituals sung on plantations, and ragtime, which was characterized by bouncing melodic piano and also developed by black musicians in the late 1800s. For years, the

Opposite: Louis Armstrong and two of his Hot Five. From left to right: Louis Armstrong, Johnny St. Cyr, and Johnny Dodds.

music was taboo, as it was associated with black people. Jazz grew in popularity as a result of recordings, the **Great Migration**, and the **Harlem Renaissance**. White Americans began to appreciate the art form and seek it out. Soon, it was a treasured cultural activity, although African Americans were still humiliated by segregation and subject to unthinkable violence during jazz's heyday. Eventually, jazz and its practitioners would help to lay the foundation for the vital civil rights movement.

Armstrong grew up alongside jazz, coming to the art form when it was in its infancy. In fact, both jazz and Louis Armstrong were born in the same city: New Orleans, Louisiana.

Armstrong has said that jazz had its origin in the church. It is certainly where he first encountered impassioned song. One very important aspect of jazz that may have been derived from church music is the four-beat, or "flat 4/4" style. This means playing a foundational meter of four beats per measure. This rhythmic timing was marked by the steady clapping of parishioners in early Baptist churches and found its way to dance halls in New Orleans. From there, it was incorporated as an essential element of jazz, and that helped swing music evolve. Jazz also tends to riff on certain phrases of music or repeat the same note with different accents. These practices also mimic the call and response of a church choir and a gospel soloist. Armstrong and other jazz enthusiasts took their inspiration from the church and shared it in dance halls, speakeasies, **honky-tonks**, and gymnasiums throughout the 1920s. While many musicians enjoyed success, very few were able to stay relevant for as long as Louis Armstrong.

Armstrong's childhood in New Orleans in the early 1900s was characterized by extreme poverty and strict segregation. He was very dark-skinned in a society that favored whiteness. Plus, he was born in one of the roughest areas of the city, nicknamed "The Battlefield." Later in life, as Armstrong moved around the city and then the country playing music, he had to be careful to plan for unforeseen circumstances that would arise as a result of racist laws. For example, there might not be a restaurant willing to serve him and his band on the road, or they might not be able to stay in the very hotel they were being paid to play at. He and his bands pursued their dreams under threats of violence and were often asked to debase themselves with racist material for the entertainment of white audiences. Later in his career, Armstrong was careful to have his white manager, Joe Glaser, on the bus whenever he toured the South.

With its street music scene and dance halls, New Orleans offered plenty of opportunities for jazz musicians to develop their skills in the Big Easy. Louis Armstrong did not take his surroundings for granted. He learned as much as he could from the cornet players whom he pestered on the streets. He used to ask musicians if he could carry their horns for them, all the while picking their brains about how to make a certain sound or perform a tricky fingering. Many of these more-accomplished horn players shrugged Armstrong off, but local cornetist Joe Oliver saw promise in the youth and indulged him. Oliver let Armstrong hold his horn, taught him tips and tricks, and even helped him get gigs.

The Louis Armstrong Memorial Statue stands in New Orleans's Louis Armstrong Park.

However, Armstrong's life in New Orleans was not without mischief, and he found himself in trouble with the law as a young man. His time at one youth home proved particularly formative and set him on a path to hone his musical talents. After receiving instruction during this period of incarceration, he spent time playing on dance boats floating down the Mississippi, making ends meet by working odd jobs and playing gigs. Eventually, Armstrong developed his talent enough to leave his home city and make a name for himself elsewhere.

At seventeen years old, Armstrong participated in the Great Migration and made his way to Chicago to pursue greater opportunity in the Windy City. African Americans had been traveling north to escape slavery for decades, but as early as 1916, a mounting number of black Americans began to move out of the South and into cities in the northeast, midwest, and western United States. More than six million African Americans relocated between 1916 and 1970. Factory jobs in northern cities paid about three times what a black worker tending land in the rural South could make. As a result, the North's metropolitan areas saw their black populations double and triple. While 90 percent of the black population in America lived in the South in 1910, by 1919, one million African Americans had relocated north of the Mason-Dixon Line.

World War I ended in the last months of 1918. Many returning African American soldiers settled in cities upon their arrival back in the country. This shift in population, combined with the three years of steadily increasing numbers of African Americans moving north, led to New York City having one of the largest black populations in the country. The majority of New York's population resided in the Harlem neighborhood. Not only did New York City have a large black population, but some of the greatest African American thinkers, writers, and artists lived in Harlem at the time. Zora Neale Hurston, Langston Hughes, Claude McKay, Countee Cullen, and W. E. B. Dubois were all located in Harlem during the Harlem Renaissance. The term "Harlem Renaissance" refers to that period in Harlem between the end of World War I and the mid-1930s when the New York neighborhood led an age of emerging black artists, musicians, and writers. These individuals made work that explored what it meant to be both black and American. Louis Armstrong contributed to this movement as well, moving to the city in 1924 for a time and then returning in 1929 at the height of the era.

As the Roaring Twenties came to a close, Louis Armstrong was busy performing in a hit Broadway musical and playing gigs in Harlem. However, many other Americans found themselves on the brink of financial collapse as US stock markets crashed and ushered in the **Great Depression**. From the end of 1929 until the late 1930s, many Americans struggled to make ends meet, and the world fell into an economic slump. Armstrong, on the other hand, managed to turn himself into an international musician, television, and film star.

Armstrong performs in the 1936 film *Pennies from Heaven.*

Armstrong stayed relevant through World War II by changing with the times. In the mid-1930s, swing music rose to popularity and was the dance craze of American youth throughout the war. Armstrong had helped to lay the foundation for the big band sound with his swinging rhythms on his cornet, and later his trumpet. Armstrong played back-to-back concerts in gymnasiums full of soldiers both black and white. When the war began to wind down, so did the country's fascination with big band swing. Again, Armstrong changed his musical focus and remained one of the most celebrated musicians in the country by giving the people what they wanted. There had been a renewed interest in traditional jazz music that had ruled the 1920s, music that Armstrong had helped create. His manager got rid of the big band Armstrong had been playing with and formed a small six-piece band. Louis Armstrong and His All Stars would be the band Louis Armstrong played with for the remainder of his life. Its changing roster included a slew of jazz legends.

No matter when or what he was playing, Louis Armstrong was able to succeed not just through his innovative playing but by connecting with his audiences, no matter who he was playing for. He played with dozens of bands, from Joe Oliver's Creole Jazz Band to Fletcher Henderson's orchestra to his Hot Five, Hot Seven, and All Star groups. Armstrong also collaborated with other gifted musicians such as Ella Fitzgerald, Bessie Smith, and Duke Ellington. He toured restlessly, playing a whopping average of three hundred concerts annually—sometimes performing one show after the other to accommodate both black and white audiences under the rule of segregation. He enjoyed international fame later in his career and became "Ambassador Satch," sharing American jazz during the height of his overseas touring.

In addition to his career playing onstage, Armstrong also appeared in over thirty films and made dozens of television performances on shows like *The Tonight Show Starring Johnny*

Armstrong pauses in between songs at a concert in Africa during his 1960 tour.

Carson, among others. Armstrong also hosted radio programs and special televised performances. He received a Grammy for Lifetime Achievement in 1972, and a number of his hits have been inducted into the Grammy Hall of Fame as foundational pieces of American music. Armstrong enjoyed massive success in his professional life, but he often struggled to maintain a stable personal life.

Louis Armstrong was married four times and was not a faithful husband to any of his wives. In fact, he was proud to declare that the most important thing in his life was his horn, regardless of whatever other relationships occupied his time. His first wife, Daisy, was a prostitute who he'd met as a young man in New Orleans. Armstrong and Daisy had a violent marriage that was eventually dissolved while Armstrong was living in Chicago in the 1920s. The divorce was obtained so Armstrong could marry Lillian Hardin, a beautiful fellow musician who urged him to develop his craft and strike out on his own. They separated in 1931, and by that time, he had already begun seeing the woman who would become his third wife, Alpha Smith. He and Hardin divorced in 1938 and the marriage between Armstrong and Alpha began. Armstrong blamed Alpha's interest in his money for breaking up their union, and in 1942, he married Lucille Wilson, a woman whom he had first seen dancing at the Cotton Club in New York. The two remained married for the rest of their lives and lived in a little house in Corona, Queens, when Armstrong was not touring.

Armstrong did not have children with any of his wives, but he did come to care for a young boy in New Orleans before he left for Chicago. The boy's name was Clarence, and he'd lived with Louis and Daisy in the early days of their marriage in New Orleans. One day, Clarence had a tragic accident, falling from the second story of the apartment building and hitting his head. Clarence's injuries left him mentally challenged. Louis continued to care for Clarence until the day he died.

Louis Armstrong had a unique, warm personality, a quick wit, and a grand smile. However, he also had his quirks. His mother encouraged the use of herbal laxatives for cleansing, and Armstrong was a lifelong devotee of the practice, even going so far as to advertise which brand of laxative he preferred. Armstrong also believed that marijuana served a similar function for his mental faculties.

Louis Armstrong's persona shaped him into an accomplished man. He became so famous at such an early age of American culture that one could say that he not only defined jazz and thus the direction of modern popular music, but he was also one of the first living models of celebrity in the United States. He supported the troops with tours and special performances but also used his right to protest to criticize the US government when young black American students were denied access to equal education. He was often relied upon to embody racist tropes for white audiences but also managed to inject his humanity into the material. The fact that he was able to soar to the apex of fame and talent through his singing and trumpet playing while being a dark-skinned black man born less than forty years after the Civil War's end is nothing short of amazing. In addition to being the target of extreme racism, Armstrong grew up desperately poor in an area of the city where prostitution was legal and violence was routine. Despite the celebrity status Louis Armstrong was able to reach, his beginnings in New Orleans were anything but **auspicious**.

2 Little Louis in New Orleans

"But man, I sure had a ball there growing up in New Orleans as a kid. We were poor and everything like that, but music was all around you. Music kept you rolling."

Louis Armstrong

Louis Armstrong would gain incredible fame and come to **codify** an original American art form with his musical talents. However, his life had humble beginnings in the city of New Orleans. Less than forty years after the Civil War ended, Louis Armstrong was born black and poor. He was raised in a notoriously violent section of the city, in a neighborhood known as Storyville, which was populated by prostitutes and gangsters

Opposite: Louis Armstrong at age twenty with his mother, May Ann.

who spent time in the area's numerous brothels, saloons, and gambling establishments. Armstrong saw the harsh realities of life and at a very young age developed the ability to see the beauty of his surroundings no matter how **desolate** they might seem.

As he would rise to prominence by defining America's first original art form, it is fitting that Armstrong adopted America's birthday as his own. In interviews, he proclaimed to have been a "Southern Doodle Dandy born on the Fourth of July 1900." However, Armstrong's actual birthdate was August 4, 1901. The false birthdate added to the mythology of Armstrong as a grandson of freed slaves who went on to define distinctly American music.

He was born to a fifteen-year-old named May Ann and spent the early years of his life with his grandmother, Josephine. During these years, Josephine made sure that Louis attended church services and Sunday school. These experiences first awakened the love of music in young Armstrong and would mold his style of performance. "That's where I acquired my singing tactics," Armstrong would later write, "I did a whole lot of singing in church … my heart went into every hymn I sang." He attended Baptist services as a child but was baptized at the Sacred Heart of Jesus Catholic Church on August 25, 1901.

His father, William Armstrong, was a laborer at a turpentine factory who rarely saw his son. He and May Ann had separated, reunited, and had a baby girl, Beatrice, two years after Louis's birth. For a time, they all lived together in a tiny apartment with Josephine. Eventually, the young parents would separate for good. Josephine raised the children until 1906, when they were sent to live with May Ann, who had a small place at the corner of Liberty and Perdido Streets. May Ann lived in the heart of the red-light district, exposing the young Armstrong children to sex and violence at an early age.

In 1907, at age six, Armstrong began attending the Fisk School for Boys, which was located across the street from a notorious honky-tonk called Funky Butt Hall. He got his first taste of jazz listening to the music echoing from inside as he peered through a crack in one of the rickety building's walls. Eavesdropping on Funky Butt Hall introduced Louis to some of the best cornet players New Orleans had to offer. Buddy Bolden, Bunk Johnson, and Joe Oliver all became familiar to Armstrong through that crack in the wall.

Armstrong's neighborhood was not just home to music halls. The heart of the black vice district, the streets were filled with prostitutes and pimps. Violence was unpredictable, and shootings and stabbings occurred regularly. Armstrong's mother took up with a number of men throughout Louis's childhood, men that Armstrong refers to as "stepfathers." Some were abusive. His mother would disappear periodically for days at a time and when this happened, Armstrong would stay with an uncle. Despite his mother's failings, Armstrong always looked up to her and credited her for instilling in him a good work ethic.

Armstrong's upbringing was also marred by poverty. He scavenged for discarded produce to help feed the small family and held a variety of menial jobs to earn his keep. He unloaded boats, washed dishes, sold newspapers, and worked junk wagons. At the age of seven, he began delivering coal for the Karnofsky family. Armstrong would travel around the white areas of Storyville in a coal wagon, blowing a tin horn to let patrons know the wagon had arrived. A family of Russian Jewish immigrants, the Karnofskys instilled a love for Jewish people in Armstrong. They fed Louis dinner at the end of his shifts and taught him Russian lullabies. It was the Karnofskys who helped Armstrong obtain his first proper musical instrument. At fifteen, Armstrong spotted a cornet in a pawnshop window. With a loan from the Karnofskys, Louis was able to buy the little cornet. Armstrong would never forget the kindness of the Karnofskys and wore a Star of David throughout his adult life as a symbol of his love for the family that offered him so much childhood support.

Though Armstrong was exposed to crushing poverty and violence as a child, he treasured his city and formed relationships with a variety of people through his music. New Orleans was an excellent city for a young musician to grow up in. With vibrant parades featuring agile marching bands and a thriving culture of street musicians blending Creole influences and the soul of the blues, New Orleans held musicians in high esteem. Armstrong reveled in the street music scene. Even after obtaining fame and glory as a professional musician, Louis reflected fondly on some of the men who had inspired him on the streets of New Orleans. In early autobiographical writings, he remembered a man named

Larenzo who collected old clothing and bottles for resale and attracted people to him by playing music from a tin horn without a mouthpiece. Larenzo talked with Armstrong about music and gave the young man a lesson in soul. Larenzo was one of many musicians to influence and educate young Louis.

Eventually, Armstrong would forsake his formal education for instruction from the New Orleans music scene. At the age of eleven, he left school and formed a vocal quartet. He and three other boys sang popular songs for tips. Flush gamblers and hustlers paid in pennies for their barbershop harmonies. Armstrong spent his days soaking in the jazz culture and getting into trouble. He had several run-ins with the law and would eventually be incarcerated for a time, but his stint in jail would only bring him closer to his music.

On January 2, 1913, Louis Armstrong got his first mention in a New Orleans newspaper, but not in recognition of his musical talents. Caught up in the celebration of New Year's Eve, Armstrong had fired his stepfather's gun in public. The *Times-Democrat* referenced his arrest as "the most serious case" of the evening. The paper also referred to Armstrong as "an old offender," though Armstrong was not yet twelve years old. He was sentenced to live in the Colored Waif's Home for Boys.

While Armstrong was terrified to leave his life of freedom on the streets of New Orleans, his time in the home would give him the discipline he desperately needed in order to grow as a musician. Armstrong's new home was founded by an ex-cavalryman, Captain

Joseph Jones, who ran the Waif's Home like a military institution. The children woke to the sound of a bugle and spent the day performing drills, cleaning, and learning carpentry, music, and gardening. The home was located just outside the city's outskirts, and the rigorous schedule along with the pastoral setting helped restless boys learn to read and write. Armstrong would grow to appreciate his new accommodations, largely because he was able to play in his first marching band.

The Waif's Home band was known as the Maple Leaf Band and was directed by Peter Davis. Davis knew how violent and impoverished Armstrong's neighborhood was. He initially doubted whether Armstrong would be a positive addition to the band and brought him in slowly, starting him on the tambourine. From there, Davis had him play a snare drum and then an alto horn. From the alto horn, Davis gave Armstrong a bugle, and when he proved himself at bugle, Davis coached him at the cornet.

Armstrong grew into an accomplished cornet player and a confident bandleader during his time at the home. He surprised all the residents of his old neighborhood when he marched through the streets playing cornet at the front of the band. All his old neighbors came down to the street to see him play. They passed a hat around, filling it with donations from the crowd. At the end of the day, the band had raised enough money to pay for new instruments and uniforms.

Armstrong left the home in June 1914 with a firm foundation in music as a result of Davis's **tutelage**. He would continue to

Armstrong sits at the top center in this photo (*see arrow*) of the Colored Waif's Home Band.

revel in the New Orleans jazz scene and seek a new mentor, one who would eventually give him the opportunity to earn a living with his talent.

At the age of thirteen, Armstrong was released into a city teeming with live music. The young musician was put in his father's custody but was soon back with May Ann and Beatrice at Liberty and Perdido. He had grown close to Peter Davis during his time in the home, and upon his release he sought another male role model to show him the way to master his instrument. He continued to sing in a vocal quartet on the street and began playing cornet in honky-tonks, dance halls, and bars. The clientele at these establishments was rough and notorious. Armstrong would typically start his set at 8:00 p.m. and play until just before daybreak, at which point he would have a drink with his fellow musicians. After a while, older, accomplished musicians began to take notice of little Louis Armstrong. They marveled at the kid playing cornet with such power and began to give him nicknames like Rhythm Jaws and Dippermouth.

Jazz musician Pops Foster brought him on as a substitute cornet player for the advertising wagon, which rode through the streets and stopped every few blocks publicizing that night's show. Armstrong played well, and the band brought him along to that night's gig where he played the blues for hustlers and prostitutes who tossed him coins. The first night, Armstrong made fifteen cents, but what the job lacked in pay it made up for in experience.

Armstrong continued to work odd jobs like delivering coal for the Karnofskys, and he played cornet for audiences as often as he could. When he wasn't playing, Armstrong was frequenting honky-tonks as a patron with a friend he'd met at the Waif's Home. They bounced from dance halls to bars, soaking in a variety of performers. "We wanted to learn all we could about life," said Armstrong. "Mostly music. We could always look forward to seeing and hearing some new piano player, with something new on the ball. Some guy who probably came from some levee camp … sit on the piano stool and beat out some of the damndest blues you've ever heard in your life."

While Louis Armstrong was trying to find his way as a professional musician, Joe Oliver made enough money from jazz that he didn't have a day job. Oliver was playing at a club called Pete LaLa's. The woman who lived next door to the club received deliveries from the Karnofskys, and when Armstrong was working, he would linger in the doorway listening to Oliver blow. Armstrong was not shy about his admiration for Oliver, and when he saw his idol in the street, he would ask to carry his horn and for any advice he had. Though Oliver had a steady career and did not need to take Armstrong under his wing, young Armstrong impressed him. Oliver began to stop by the honky-tonks where Armstrong played after finishing his own gigs. The prostitutes and hustlers were delighted to see Joe Oliver demonstrate little tricks for Armstrong. In exchange for cornet lessons, Armstrong would

Armstrong's beloved mentor, Joe Oliver, circa 1915

run errands for Oliver's wife, Stella. Oliver often had Armstrong over for dinner, and the two became very close.

It made sense that Joe Oliver ended up mentoring Louis Armstrong, as the two had a lot in common. Both fell in love with church music as children. Both were praised initially for their skill in playing the blues. They both had very dark skin and came from fractured families. Oliver was not just a musical mentor but also the father figure Armstrong needed in his teenage years. Oliver helped Armstrong find jobs, gave him his old cornet, and advised him when he got into trouble. Armstrong called Oliver "Papa." Oliver also must have seen something of himself in the young musician with whom he seemed to share so much.

Oliver was most admired for playing a unique kind of New Orleans jazz referred to as "freak music." Freak music highlighted the musician's ability to manipulate the tone of the instrument. Crowds gathered to hear Oliver use an assortment of objects to bend the sound of his cornet. He used beer buckets, toilet plungers, even coconuts to create effects that approximated the human voice. He would use techniques such as half-valving, flutter-tonguing, growls, and a subtle change in the tension of his lips to amplify his sounds. Oliver was also excellent when it came to improvisation. Armstrong learned many of his solos from watching Oliver play. Being able to directly observe his mentor in combination with the instruction he received from Oliver offered Armstrong an invaluable education.

Kid Ory was a musician and manager in New Orleans; he had a band that he sometimes played in and other times just booked gigs and advertised for. Around 1917, Joe Oliver joined Kid Ory's Band and was a natural leader, so much so that Ory began promoting the band as the "Ory and Oliver Band." During that same time, Armstrong formed a six-piece band modeled after Ory and Oliver's band and played in various honky-tonks. Eventually, Armstrong's band broke up, but Armstrong continued to play for advertising wagons and imitate Oliver while working as many odd jobs as he could.

Meanwhile, in November 1917, a worldwide flu pandemic swept across the United States. Officials closed dance halls to stem the spread of disease. With live music only being offered during limited hours, paying gigs for musicians began to dry up. In addition to the flu, the Great Migration began to drain Southern cities of black citizens who moved north in search of greater opportunity. Joe Oliver was among those who left New Orleans, settling in Chicago in 1918. Ory labored over who Oliver's replacement would be, but the remaining members of the band convinced him: it was Armstrong who knew Oliver's solos and had been imitating not just Oliver's style but Kid Ory's band with a six-piece outfit of his own. Ory acquiesced and offered Armstrong the position. Louis Armstrong would follow in his mentor's footsteps.

Louis Armstrong may have come of age in a rough neighborhood, but he managed to see the beauty of his surroundings and worked hard to support his family. Despite getting into trouble with the law and dropping out of school, Armstrong used his time in the Waif's Home to better himself. He developed a basic musical education from Peter Davis and Joe Oliver, eventually managing to play paid gigs. He learned quickly the daily grind of trying to make it as a professional musician. Oliver's departure from the city in 1918 allowed Armstrong his first big break as leader of the Kid Ory Band. As the years progressed, Armstrong would continue to play with the Kid Ory Band while getting his first taste of working as a traveling musician.

3 From the Big Easy to the Big City

"My boyhood dream had come true at last."

Louis Armstrong writing about his first night playing in Chicago with Joe Oliver's Creole Jazz Band

By the age of seventeen, Louis Armstrong had survived the **torrid** streets of New Orleans and managed to get by despite impoverished circumstances. He had discovered a love of music in church and in the streets—where he also found trouble. A stint in the Colored Waif's Home offered him a more formal music education than he had gotten while freewheeling around New Orleans. A few years later, Armstrong would be making a living with his horn and getting a glimpse of how far his talent could take him.

Opposite: Kid Ory (pictured here) gave Armstrong one of his first big breaks with a spot in his band.

In 1918, Armstrong found himself at the head of the Kid Ory Band. Armstrong's confidence increased after he grew accustomed to playing in Ory's band. His playing speed picked up, and his powerful horn dazzled audiences. Other bands recruited him to play on nights when he wasn't playing for Kid Ory. Steadily, Armstrong made himself a home playing professionally in New Orleans. He reflected fondly on his time in one of his many memoirs:

> *I was really stickin' with cash. Because our tips from those prosperous prostitutes, who came to our joint, gave us lots of tips to play different tunes for them and their Johns … we made good tips—that is, as far as tips go—for a barrel house honky-tonk. Where nothing but the lowest of guys comes into town on payday looking for anything to happen. And believe me, it did. And I was right in the middle of it all. With not a thing on my mind but my cornet-piano-drums to look forward to every night. And I loved it. In fact, I did not know of anything else. And did not want to think of anything else. I was perfectly happy. That was my life and that was that. And I'll gladly live it all over again, so help me.*

The same year Armstrong took his place in Ory's band, he would also marry his first wife, a prostitute named Daisy. Daisy was a violent woman who Armstrong called "the prettiest and baddest whore in Gretna, Louisiana." They wed early in the year and began to fight immediately. Daisy found a weak spot on Armstrong when she noticed that she could upset him by hitting him in the mouth, potentially upsetting his career in music. She and Armstrong had a volatile relationship, to say the least, and while things were going well for his music, he began to contemplate escaping Daisy.

As his star continued to rise, Armstrong got offers from several different musicians and managers. Fate Marable, a bandleader who played on steam riverboats that floated up and down the Mississippi River, made Armstrong one such offer. Marable had seen Armstrong play and offered him a gig on these excursion boats. Fletcher Henderson, a New York City bandleader, also showed an interest in Armstrong, but Louis was nervous about leaving New Orleans. He had heard terrifying stories of traveling for musical gigs and ending up stranded in an area that was particularly unfriendly to African Americans. This fear was more than reasonable, as lynching was still a common practice in both the North and the South and the Ku Klux Klan was on the rise nationwide. Marable's offer did carry some sense of safety in that anyone could see the boats leave the dock on Canal Street and return regularly on a schedule.

In addition to being swayed by the idea of leaving New Orleans without actually leaving his beloved city for good, Armstrong had another reason for considering Marable's offer. Though he had been playing as a full-time cornetist, he could not read music. He knew it was necessary to learn and that if he played for Marable he would have to learn. Armstrong reflected on the proposition later: "I jumped at the opportunity, because I thought it was an advancement towards my musical career … Fate's band had to read, and they did read music, perfectly. And Ory's band didn't."

In the fall of 1918, Armstrong made arrangements to cut his time with the Kid Ory band in order to take Marable up on his offer. Aboard the riverboats, he took his musical prowess to the next level under a disciplined schedule that would rival that of his time in the Waif's Home. In the summer of 1919, Louis Armstrong took his first steps outside of his birth city to Saint Louis, Missouri.

Marable's bands played on riverboats owned by Captain John Streckfus, a fiddle player. He began offering rides on his dancer riverboats in 1901, and soon the trend gained more interest.

Armstrong traveled by train to St. Louis, the Streckfus line's home base. David Jones, a mellophone player, was charged with looking after him, and while they did not bond during the trip, the two eventually became good friends. Seventeen-year-old Armstrong was so astonished at the big buildings in St. Louis that he asked if they were colleges.

After arriving at their destination, Armstrong met the group he'd be playing with. There was Warren "Baby" Dodds on the drums, Johnny St. Cyr on banjo, and Pops Foster on bass. Working out of Saint Louis demanded long hours from the musicians. They started on the SS *Sidney* at 9:00 a.m. and returned at

6:00 p.m. They got a break for dinner and then played another trip at 8:30 p.m., called "the moonlight ride." The musicians would also play on the dock to advertise the excursions. Altogether, they ended up working from 8:00 a.m. to around 11:30 p.m.

Streckfus was a retired pianist who had high musical standards for his dance ships. He attended his band's rehearsals and tapped along while he looked at his watch. Expecting a tempo of seventy beats per minute for foxtrots and ninety beats per minute for one-steps, he was **livid** if the band was off. When bands struggled to keep tempo, Streckfus did not hesitate to replace members. The musicians rehearsed often and were tasked with learning fourteen new songs every two weeks.

Playing fast was not an issue for Armstrong or his new cohorts. Reading music was. Marable knew that his new musicians did not read music and was willing to teach them. He had Joe Howard, the first chair cornetist, play lead melody for Armstrong, who quickly committed it to memory and was able to add a harmony. When Howard got sick, a concerted effort was made to teach Armstrong, as he would have to take over first chair. Armstrong began working with David Jones, nicknamed Br'er Jones, every day for ninety minutes. Later in life, he would credit these lessons with granting him the ability to tap into his potential. He remembered Jones saying, "You'll never be able to swing any better than you already know how until you learn to read. Then you will swing in ways you never thought of before." Armstrong found that Jones was

Louis Armstrong played Streckfus line riverboat excursions on steamboats like this one.

right and his playing improved as his understanding of written music deepened.

While the schedule and standards were strict, trips with the Streckfus line allowed Armstrong to have several new experiences. First, he was out of New Orleans for the first time in his life, traveling to various cities in Illinois, Iowa, Louisiana, and Missouri. Late in summer when it got warm enough, they traveled as far north as Saint Paul, Minnesota. The boats were, of course, segregated, and Armstrong got his first taste of playing for white audiences who were not always appropriate. In some of the towns they stopped in, he and his bandmates were the first black people that the white people living there had seen play European instruments. They stared, and sometimes a member of the crowd would heckle the musicians. The band was forbidden to talk to the white spectators and was separated from the crowd by a railing onboard the SS *Sidney*. Streckfus reserved Monday nights for African American customers, and on these nights the band was able to drink, smoke, and socialize with the audience. Second, Armstrong was also making more money than he ever had. If he kept to the rigid schedule and followed the rules, he was rewarded with $37.50 every week, plus room and board, and a weekly bonus of $5 paid at the end of each cruise. He was making twice what Kid Ory paid him and playing alongside the best musicians New Orleans had to offer.

Not only was Armstrong enjoying his time on the riverboat during the summer months, but his experiences would also benefit him in the winter when he was back in New Orleans. As he traveled around playing, more and more people heard his music, and interest in the young cornetist grew. He was offered a **lucrative** position playing in Tom Anderson's New Cabaret, a place just outside Storyville. Armstrong remembered this period of his life as one of great mobility: "I made so much money I didn't know what to do with it." In 1921, he became a permanent member of the Tuxedo Brass Band, an elite marching band in New Orleans.

After three summers of playing with Fate Marable, Armstrong quit. He remained tightlipped about his parting with Marable throughout his life. However, Warren Dodds, the drummer who played with Armstrong in Marable's band, later said that he and Armstrong quit because they didn't want to be limited to playing Streckfus's strict dance band tempos. Another source claimed that Armstrong was fired for fighting onboard. Marable claimed that Armstrong refused to continue his after-hours practice routine. In any case, after three years, Armstrong stopped playing the riverboat excursions. Even though he had stopped working for Marable, Armstrong recognized how much his playing had improved. In 1936, he wrote:

> *I could read music very well by now and was getting hotter and hotter ... My chest had filled out deeper and my lips and jaws had got stronger, so I could blow much harder and longer than before without getting tired. I had made a special point of the high register, and was beginning to make my high-C notes more and more often.*

During his time in Saint Louis, Oliver had come to visit Armstrong for four days and attempted to convince his protégé to come to Chicago. Armstrong declined the invitation at the time, but before long, he did make his way north to join his mentor. Joe Oliver's Creole Jazz Band was becoming very popular and opened at Chicago's Lincoln Gardens earlier that summer. Oliver was looking to bring on a second cornet player to ease the burden of playing so much. He sent a telegram to Armstrong along with a one-way train ticket. On August 8, 1922, Armstrong played a funeral with the Tuxedo Band, donned a pair of long underwear at the request of May Ann, who feared it would be frigid there despite it being late summer, and boarded the Illinois Central Railroad headed for Chicago.

Though Armstrong had decided to leave his beloved city, he was still nervous about moving. "I always was afraid to leave home because so many of the boys from home had gone up North and came back in such bad shape," Armstrong wrote later in life. However, Chicago offered Armstrong the opportunity to make even more money. Oliver had offered him $52 every week, much more than he had made back home or on the riverboats. Chicago also offered Armstrong the chance to prove himself in a city he hadn't grown up in. Many of the older professional musicians in New Orleans thought he played well but saw him as "Little Louis" despite his accomplished playing and 226-pound (102-kilogram) frame. The benefits of moving to Chicago far outweighed his fears of leaving New Orleans. Even if Armstrong was far from home, he didn't feel it, as he was playing with his childhood mentor and other musicians he already knew. Baby Dodds and his brother Johnny, who had also worked for Fate Marable aboard the riverboats, were already playing with Oliver's band. Joe Oliver and his wife Stella took Louis into a community of black New Orleanians who had come to Chicago in search of greater mobility.

King Oliver's Creole Jazz Band. Armstrong kneels in front, Lil Hardin sits at the piano, and Joe Oliver stands in the back center.

Armstrong was still a bit overwhelmed by the city's huge skyscrapers. Oliver had paid a porter to direct his new cornet player to Lincoln Gardens. The porter greeted Armstrong, saying, "You are the young man who's to join King Oliver's band." In New Orleans, Oliver was known as Joe. His mentor's ascent to royalty in this busy new city further disoriented Armstrong. Upon making his way to Lincoln Gardens, he lingered in the doorway, listening to the rehearsal until Oliver barked at him to come in. Armstrong was, in a sense, home.

After rehearsal, Oliver took Armstrong to his apartment, where Stella prepared Armstrong's favorite meal: red beans and rice. Then Oliver took Armstrong to the boardinghouse where he'd arranged for Armstrong to stay; Armstrong was astonished by the luxury of having a private bathroom. That night, he played for the first time with Oliver's Creole Jazz Band at Lincoln Gardens. As the night of music drew to a close, a member of the audience shouted, "Let the youngster blow!" prompting Louis Armstrong to play his first solo in Chicago.

Not only did Chicago bring change to his professional life. It brought significant change to his personal life as well. In 1922, he met Lillian Hardin, an educated fellow musician who was also a recent addition to Oliver's band. Little did he know it upon first meeting her, but this woman would take notice of Armstrong and change his life forever.

4 The Windy City and the Big Apple

> ***"I have been always Crazy over Joe Oliver and his playing. So when Joe sent for me to join him in Chicago I was happy because I know I'd feel at home and he'd see after me."***
>
> **Louis Armstrong**

In 1922, Louis Armstrong found himself reunited with his childhood mentor in Chicago, Illinois. Joe Oliver's Creole Jazz Band offered Armstrong the chance to play alongside his idol and other New Orleans musicians who he had played with back home. One member new to Armstrong was the slender, attractive, Fisk-educated pianist Lillian "Lil" Hardin. Although Hardin was not initially attracted to Armstrong, he was taken with her.

Opposite: Portrait of Lillian "Lil" Hardin, Armstrong's second wife and fellow band member

For a while after arriving, Armstrong was having the time of his life. He played the music he loved with the man he most loved to play with and made the most money he'd made in his life. In April 1923, the Creole Jazz Band took a train to Richmond, Indiana, the home of Gennett Records. There they recorded "Chimes Blues." Armstrong's passionate solo work gave listeners a taste of the future of jazz. His playing was reportedly so powerful that he had to stand in the hallway and play while the other musicians played closer to the microphone. Armstrong's playing was as captivating on record as it was at Lincoln Gardens where scores of Chicagoans flocked to hear the young cornet player blow.

After seeing the stir Armstrong's playing caused among the Chicago crowds, Hardin grew more curious about the New Orleans transplant. That curiosity soon blossomed into romance as the two began meeting for breakfasts and dinners at the Dreamland Café. Hardin had separated from her husband, singer Jimmie Johnson, shortly after Armstrong had arrived in Chicago, but Louis was still legally married to Daisy. In 1923, Hardin arranged both of their divorces, and the two wed on February 5, 1924. As Armstrong's wife, Lil put all her efforts into encouraging Louis to make a name for himself.

Lillian Hardin was not the only person who thought Armstrong could lead his own band. Once Armstrong began playing with the Creole Jazz Band, Chicagoans who frequented Lincoln Gardens spread the word about the talented new arrival. On his first night of playing, audience members were calling for solos. His nimble fingers, strong lips, and expansive lungs let him play faster, louder, and higher, yet he was relegated to playing second chair.

While Oliver mentored Armstrong throughout his life, he was still the bandleader and had no interest in being outperformed. Though Armstrong tried not to overtake Oliver's playing with the sound of his own horn, the buzz about Armstrong's playing weighed on Oliver. He was concerned about being outshone by his former pupil, and so he reasoned, "As long as I keep him with me, he won't be able to get ahead of me."

During their courtship, Lil had discovered that Oliver was being less than honest about the money Louis was making each week. One day she commented on Louis's wardrobe, which was secondhand, and asked him where his money was. Armstrong explained, "Joe keeps my money." After this exchange, Hardin swore she would look after Louis. Oliver could do no wrong in the eyes of his former child prodigy, but not even Louis could ignore the tensions that developed within the Creole Jazz Band. Eventually, Dodds confronted Oliver about cheating the band members, Oliver refused to show them the royalty checks he received from Gennett, and everyone except Louis and Lil quit the band. Shortly after they married, Lil was finally able to convince Louis to leave Oliver, saying, "You can't be married to Joe and to me." Joe Oliver and Louis Armstrong parted amicably despite Oliver's underhanded tactics.

Through Lil's influence, Armstrong soon started playing at Dreamland Café with Ollie Powers, a singing drummer. Louis was the only cornet in the band, and because he was no longer following a lead horn, Armstrong shone much brighter. Not long after he began playing at Dreamland, Armstrong was contacted once again by Fletcher Henderson. He was the leader of Harlem's most famous dance orchestra, which played at Roseland Ballroom in New York City. Henderson sent a telegram asking Armstrong to join the most elite group of African American musicians at a time when jazz was sweeping the nation.

With Lil's encouragement and an offer he couldn't refuse, Armstrong made his way to the East Coast without his wife. Lil stayed behind in Chicago, playing Dreamland, and visited New York when she got the chance.

When Louis Armstrong made his way to New York City in 1924, the Harlem Renaissance was in full swing. The Great Migration had made it a popular destination among Southern blacks seeking greater opportunity. African American culture caught mainstream attention as innovative writers, intellectuals, artists, and musicians emerged. Black editors and writers published poetry and prose that explored the experience of being an African American. Langston Hughes, one of the period's most notable poets, began publishing his poetry three years prior to Armstrong's arrival. Poets like Countee Cullen and Claude McKay also spent time in Harlem and published vital works. Intellectuals such as W. E. B. Du Bois, Alain Locke, and Marcus Garvey contributed ideas about what black identity meant. Black musicians were also being celebrated at this time.

Fletcher Henderson's own reputation as an innovative, polished musician was well established. His orchestra played Roseland Ballroom in the heart of Manhattan. Roseland also happened to be a main attraction for white dancers. Though he would play live for mostly all white audiences, Armstrong changed the way New York listened to jazz and contributed his voice to the explosion of black art centered in Harlem.

Armstrong's time in Henderson's orchestra was challenging and disciplined, but his experiences playing at the Waif's Home and on riverboat excursions had prepared him for Henderson's expectations.

Henderson's dance orchestra played for white dancers. The standards for their playing were strict, as white audiences enjoyed jazz but were uncomfortable with music that was "too black." The band members were expected to be able to sight-read musical arrangements and played a mix of popular songs, classical tunes, and jazz-inspired instrumentals. Armstrong once again had to develop his music-reading skills, as Henderson's arrangements were more complex and written in several different keys.

In his first rehearsals, Armstrong made several mistakes but caught on quickly. He felt somewhat out of place among his new colleagues, who were more sophisticated in terms of dress, but it was his playing that truly set him apart.

A week after Armstrong arrived in New York, Henderson's band went into the recording studio. They played Don Redman's "Shanghai Shuffle," and Armstrong's mark on it is unmistakable. In

Louis Armstrong with the Fletcher Henderson Band. Fletcher Henderson sits at the piano, and Armstrong stands in the back center.

the piece, the orchestra bounces along as Armstrong blazes into a chorus where he plays eighteen Cs, one after the other. While the note does not vary, Armstrong accents his playing in such a way that his chorus is enlivened through his energetic, changing rhythm. No one had ever played like this, but Armstrong's phrasing and passionate solos would become the common language of jazz.

Not only were Armstrong's solos making impressions on audiences at Roseland Ballroom and on listeners who heard his recordings with Henderson's orchestra, but the Creole Jazz Band's records were also circulating Harlem. Through this, Armstrong gained some confidence knowing that his playing was earning him a wider reputation. His choruses transformed the orchestra, and Don Redman, Henderson's arranger, began to write music that highlighted Armstrong's powerful cornet. Rex Stewart, a fellow cornet player who joined the band in 1926, wrote, "From the time Louis catapulted onto the New York scene, everybody and their brother tried to play like him." Henderson even encouraged new band members to "play like Louis" and referred to his swinging style of playing as Armstrong's "New Orleans punch and bounce."

Louis Armstrong took New York by storm as he continued to play Roseland and make recordings set up by Frank Walker, head of Columbia's race records, and Clarence Williams, a New Orleans pianist and an old friend of Louis's. Armstrong played accompaniment for a number of blues singers including Bessie Smith, Ma Rainey, and lesser-known artists like Maggie Jones and Virginia Liston. Armstrong also recorded duets with Sidney Bechet for Gennett and OKeh Records. Bechet had played with a number of musicians in New Orleans when Armstrong was a child, including his mentor Joe Oliver. In tunes like "Texas Moaner Blues" and "Cake Walkin' Babies from Home," listeners can hear the fervor of Armstrong's performance alongside a worthy rival on the horn. As Louis Armstrong began to clearly define his solo style, he also grew restless in Fletcher Henderson's band.

Armstrong was good-natured, took his music seriously, and was committed to developing his skills by learning as much as he could about playing. However, his fellow orchestra members were not as dedicated to their practice, and it showed in their tardiness to rehearsal and sloppy approach. Hard drinking affected some of his colleagues' performances, and Armstrong grew frustrated with his fellow musicians. He also wanted to do more singing, but Henderson rarely allowed him the opportunity. At the same time, Lil was encouraging him to come back to Chicago. She had visited Armstrong to see him play in New York and was dismayed to see that his name was not featured in advertisements featuring Fate Marable's orchestra. She was proud of the work he had done in New York but believed Armstrong deserved to have his name on the marquee. In November 1925, he went back to Dreamland Café in Chicago to play with Lil, where she **billed** him as "the World's Greatest Cornet Player."

Not only had Lil set up a band for Louis to join, but she'd also convinced the management to pay him seventy-five dollars every week, twenty dollars more than he was making playing for Fletcher Henderson. He would play Dreamland at night and record for OKeh when he got off around nine in the morning. Less than a week after the band debuted at Dreamland, Armstrong, Lil, Johnny Dodds, Kid Ory, and Johnny St. Cyr made three

In the early 1920s, Armstrong spent time playing gigs in the bustling city of Chicago.

classic recordings under the name "Louis Armstrong and His Hot Five." Among the first recordings of this historical jazz group was "Gut Bucket Blues." During the recording, Armstrong introduced each member of the band as they each played solos. Armstrong encouraged them along the way, saying things like, "Miss Lil! Whip it, kid!" and, "Blow that thing, Mr. Johnny Dodds!" Eventually, Armstrong's Hot Five group would become the Hot Seven when Warren Dodds joined on drums and Pete Briggs on tuba. Armstrong thrived as a band leader and did his best to highlight every instrument.

In February 1926, during a recording session for OKeh Records, Louis Armstrong sang on "Heebie Jeebies" and did something that jazz fans would imitate for years to come. When listeners get to the second verse they hear Armstrong improvising nonsensical rhythmic sounds instead of singing. He explained the choice with an anecdote he loved to tell:

> *I dropped the paper with the lyrics—right in the middle of the tune ... And I did not want to stop and spoil the record which was moving along so wonderfully ... So when I dropped the paper, I immediately turned back into the horn and started to* **scatting** *... When I finished the record I just knew the recording people would throw it out ... And to my surprise they all came running out of the controlling booth and said, "Leave that in."*

The record sold more than forty thousand copies, and soon musicians all over Chicago were greeting each other with Armstrong's riffs. While scat singing had been around for years,

Armstrong's interpretation was the first that many audiences had ever heard. As a result, when most jazz enthusiasts thought of scatting, they heard Armstrong's vocal improvisations.

The Hot Five and Hot Seven recordings let Armstrong stretch himself creatively. He sang and played and fronted his first band, which consisted of musicians he had been playing with for years, some since he was a child in New Orleans. The band rehearsed in Armstrong's living room and rarely wrote any music down. OKeh Records and Armstrong worked out a flat fee of fifty dollars for every side recorded. The band would record on "side A" of the record then flip it over and record "side B." This earned Armstrong and his band one hundred dollars total. Though Armstrong did not receive any royalties, the sixty-five recordings he made under his name between 1925 and 1928 came to serve as the standard of jazz and continue to be reissued today.

In addition to playing at Dreamland Café, Armstrong also joined conductor Erskine Tate's "Little Symphony," which played at the Vendome Theater, a 1,300-seat movie house with an orchestra pit. The musicians played accompaniment for the silent films as well as popular music between screenings. It was with Tate's orchestra that Armstrong began to play trumpet. He was so loved by audiences that Tate asked him to perform onstage during his solo, but Armstrong did not want to alienate his fellow musicians. As a compromise, a spotlight shone down on Armstrong as he played, to the delight of the uproarious crowds. Armstrong played high notes on his trumpet, sang, and performed short comedic routines impersonating a number of individuals, including an old-time preacher.

In April 1926, Armstrong got an offer from Joe Oliver to play at Plantation Café, another Southside club. On the way to his first rehearsal, Armstrong happened upon Earl Hines, a piano player he'd played with years before. Hines was working for Carroll Dickerson at the Sunset Café, a club right across the street from the Plantation, where Armstrong was headed. Hines teased Armstrong about playing with an old-timer like Joe Oliver, saying, "Why don't you come on over with us young fellows?" The Sunset offered Armstrong ten dollars more per week than Oliver, and with some encouragement from Lil, Louis started playing at the Sunset Café. His band was called Louis Armstrong and His Stompers.

Earl Hines and Louis Armstrong were both passionate musicians and mischievous young men. The two got along famously, and their friendship shone through in the interplay of Armstrong's horn and Hines's piano during performances by the Sunset Café band. They also made recordings together.

Personally, Armstrong's life took another turn in 1928, when he met a young woman named Alpha Smith while playing at the Vendome. By that time, he and Lil were a popular couple, but Lil always strove to make Louis achieve his best, sometimes to the point of pushing him too far. Alpha was a likeable woman. Soon after meeting, Armstrong began an affair with her. Tensions rose between Lil and Louis, as Armstrong carried on with Alpha and goofed off with other musicians during rehearsal. A few years later, the two decided to officially separate. It was not long before Alpha would become Louis's third wife.

Professionally, in June 1928, Armstrong recorded a King Oliver tune along with Hines and his Hot Five, called "West End Blues." It became one of the most well-known recordings in jazz history. Listeners raved about Armstrong's opening **cadenza** and his scat vocals. The song would come to offer a picture of the freewheeling jazz culture on the precipice of the Great Depression.

As the twenties came to a close, Armstrong was making more and more records with different artists, including his Hot Five and Hot Seven groups. However, he wanted more. His records were selling well among black audiences in the Southside of Chicago and he was playing well-attended shows, but he was largely unknown to white audiences. He wanted to change that, and in New York City, he would get his chance, on Broadway.

5 Primetime

"My whole life, my whole soul, my whole spirit is to blow that horn."

Louis Armstrong

By 1929, Louis Armstrong had played many years throughout Chicago, most recently at the Sunset Café. The club's rough clientele included heavily connected mobsters. One of these people eventually guided Armstrong back to the Big Apple.

At the Sunset Café there was regular violence, and federal agents often raided the venue. In fact, the café was getting raided on such a regular basis that Earl Hines was always on the lookout for the paddy wagon. The joke was he was always ready to race toward it in order to get a seat and not have to stand.

Opposite: Louis Armstrong (*second from the left*) and His Stompers appear at Chicago's Sunset Café in 1927.

Louis Armstrong had been in contact with Tommy Rockwell, a booking agent with mob connections, who had arranged a few recordings for him. Rockwell was trying to lure Armstrong back to the city, guaranteeing that he could make him unimaginably famous if he returned to New York as a solo artist.

Eventually, Armstrong took Rockwell up on his offer. He left for New York in the summer of 1929 but neglected to tell Rockwell that he had decided to bring his band with him. The musicians drove across the country and were amazed to hear Armstrong's records playing in gas stations and shops in black neighborhoods all the way to New York. When they finally arrived in Rockwell's office, he was furious with Armstrong for bringing the rest of his band. "Just the same, my boys are here in New York, so find something for us to do," was all Armstrong said in reply.

The first gig Armstrong and his band got was at the Audubon Theater. They filled in for Duke Ellington's band as accompaniment to Letha Hill. Louis stole the show that night with his playing on the band's signature number, "St. Louis Blues." He played so loudly and passionately that Hill kept looking back at him, distracted. When Armstrong finished, even the pit band stood up and cheered.

The band went on to open at the Savoy Ballroom and the Lafayette. In June 1929, Armstrong and his band started playing at Connie's Inn, a basement club at Seventh Avenue and West 131st Street. The club featured the best entertainers and paid them well; it was second only to Harlem's infamous Cotton Club.

There were two shows nightly, the first at midnight and the second at 2 a.m. Armstrong and the band were to play the floorshow and also provide dance music for patrons. While everyone who worked at these "black and tan" establishments was black, black customers were very rarely allowed entry. Like the clubs he'd played in Chicago, Connie's Inn had connections to illegal activity. One of Armstrong's biggest fans was part-owner and murderous gangster Dutch Schultz.

One advantage of playing New York clubs was the proximity to Broadway and the opportunity to gain fame and fortune performing in **revues**. A few weeks after opening at Connie's Inn, Armstrong got his chance to do just that in the show *Hot Chocolates*, which premiered at the Hudson Theatre on June 20, 1929. The musical revue was written by Andy Razaf, Harry Brooks, and Thomas "Fats" Waller. One of the most famous songs to be featured was a tune called "Ain't Misbehavin'." It was performed in the first act by Edith Wilson and then again as an **entr'acte**. Louis Armstrong sang the reprisal from the orchestra pit after intermission. The *New York Times* review of the opening did not mention his name but called Armstrong's performance "a highlight of the première." A month later, Armstrong recorded "Ain't Misbehavin'" for OKeh. His performance is polished from rehearsal and nightly performances, but his solos still feel spontaneous and exciting. The flip side of the record featured the song "Black and Blue," which Armstrong did not sing in *Hot Chocolates*. While the lyrics are meant to relate the tale of a dark-skinned woman whose lover is attracted to women with lighter complexions, Armstrong's singing transformed the song. Listeners heard a story, intoned with deep feeling and without self-pity, about the struggle of being black in a society that favored and was run by whites.

Around the same time, Armstrong recorded a number of Tin Pan Alley tunes. These songs defined the beginnings of the US music industry in the late nineteenth and early twentieth centuries. They were part of a well-known, if limited, canon of popular music at the time. Armstrong sang songs like "I'm Confessin' (That I Love You)," "Star Dust," "I Can't Give You Anything But Love (Baby)," and "Lazy River," bringing his signature interpretation to songs that listeners were already familiar with. Armstrong's recordings were anything but monotonous; New York audiences couldn't get enough of him. He certainly gave them a wealth of opportunities to catch him: for the rest of the year, he shuffled from Broadway back to Harlem to play at Connie's Inn. Armstrong even worked in several performances at the Lafayette.

While *Hot Chocolates* did not make Louis Armstrong a household name among white audiences, he was known for the song "Ain't Misbehavin'," which he performed for years. Later in life, Armstrong reflected on the popularity the song had afforded him: "I believe that great song, and the chance I got to play it, did a lot to make me better known all over the country."

Armstrong's audiences were diversifying. Not only was he becoming as famous in New York as he had been in Chicago among black listeners, but he was being appreciated by white musicians as well. In a gesture of admiration, a number of white

The cover image of sheet music for "Ain't Misbehavin' (I'm Savin' My Love For You)" from the musical *Hot Chocolates* by Andy Razaf, Thomas Waller, and Harry Brooks

musicians threw a banquet in his honor and gave him an engraved wristwatch, which reportedly read: "To Louis Armstrong, the World's Greatest Cornetist, from the Musicians of New York." Since black and white musicians were not allowed to play together publicly, the tribute was especially poignant.

On October 29, 1929, the United States stock market crashed, and Americans began to struggle through the Great Depression. Jazz musicians were no exception. Fletcher Henderson's band separated. King Oliver recorded songs but had a hard time making ends meet. Sidney Bechet eventually moved to Paris, supporting himself by making alterations to clothing, and Kid Ory made his way back to New Orleans, where he kept chickens. The Cotton Club, New York's most famous black and tan establishment, struggled for years and finally closed its doors in 1936.

While others struggled, Louis Armstrong was as busy as he had ever been. In 1929, the band he had come to New York with was fired from the gig at Connie's Inn for drinking on the job. However, Tommy Rockwell made plans for Armstrong to go out on his own. For the first half of 1930, Armstrong toured as a single act, supported by a number of different bands. Upon his return to New York, he was surprised to find that white press outlets had begun to cover his comings and goings. In his Broadway column, Walter Winchell wrote, "Louis Armstrong, the most torrid of the horn-tooters and blues-shooers, is at the Cocoanut Grove and his delightful specialties serve to entice the bored-with-Broadway diversion seekers … Armstrong offers an endless routine of terrifically-tempoed tunes." By the end of the year, Louis Armstrong was on the other side of the country, in Culver City just outside Los Angeles, California.

Armstrong went from captivating the East Coast crowds with his swinging trumpet to rubbing elbows with Hollywood. He started playing at Frank Sebastian's New Cotton Club along with talented young drummer Lionel Hampton. Armstrong's playing was broadcast for fans who couldn't afford the Cotton Club, and Californians were thrilled. Soon, he began receiving movie offers. His first movie appearance was in a 1930 film called *Ex-Flame*.

The 1930s would yield a slew of memorable songs for Armstrong. This included "Blue Yodel Number Nine," his last recording as a **sideman**, backing Jimmie Rodgers. Records like "I'm A Ding Dong Daddy from Dumas," "Shine," and "Memories of You" gained popularity.

Along with these hits, Armstrong introduced new concepts and styles to jazz. For instance, while recording "Memories of You," Lionel Hampton found a vibraphone in the studio. He and Armstrong decided to use it in the song's opening. It was the first time a vibraphone solo was featured on a jazz record.

During this time, Armstrong also began playing **ballads** seriously. "Body and Soul" and "If We Never Meet Again" are testaments to his skill. Armstrong befriended Hollywood stars such as Bing Crosby and began to experience some of the perks of being an American celebrity.

Louis Armstrong was a musical genius but did have faults that led him down darker paths. One of his vices was smoking marijuana. He especially indulged before gigs and recording sessions. In November 1930, he found himself arrested, along with drummer Vic Berton, for smoking a joint on a break in the parking lot of the Cotton Club. They were each sentenced to six

Bing Crosby (*left*) and Louis Armstrong (*right*) shared a mutual admiration for each other's music.

months in jail, along with a one thousand dollar fine. Armstrong was able to avoid the harshest terms of his sentence. However, the arrest only fueled his ascent to stardom.

Despite the brush with the law, California treated Louis Armstrong well. He played to radio and live audiences in a lavish club attended by Hollywood stars who the Great Depression had not dimmed. Armstrong influenced up-and-coming **crooner** Bing Crosby, a regular at his shows. He enjoyed an artistic kinship with Lionel Hampton and the satisfaction of knowing his music was being heard on both coasts. In the spring of 1931, Armstrong ended his gig at the Cotton Club and made his way back to Chicago.

Johnny Collins was managing Armstrong at that time and demanding a significant percentage of his weekly pay. Collins claimed to be a messenger of Tommy Rockwell and got him a gig at the Regal Theater. Chicago was surprised by Armstrong's reemergence as news of his arrest and sentencing had spread, but the Windy City was happy to have him back. In April 1931, Armstrong recorded several more songs, including "When Your Lover Has Gone," "Wrap Your Troubles in Dreams," "World on a String," "Sleepy Time Down South," and many more. Many of these newly recorded tunes would come to **epitomize** Armstrong's distinct style.

Armstrong went right back to playing live after finishing the recordings. Collins had a gig lined up at the Showboat, a nightclub that had a reputation of being a local mob hangout. His opening night was broadcast on WIBC and featured several white bandleaders taking turns saying "a few words in favor of Louie Armstrong."

There was a violent side to the Showboat. It served as a bookie joint for a number of gangsters, and huge amounts of cash passed through the club on a nightly basis. Armstrong started receiving blackmail threats as soon as he started playing at the Showboat. Two men were arrested for attempting to extort Armstrong, but his run-ins with criminals were far from over.

The Showboat was a notoriously rough club where gangsters fought on the dance floor, but Armstrong had seen mayhem like this from his days in New Orleans. One night a man broke a chair over a woman's head, and though the splintered shards hit Armstrong's horn, he continued to play. He experienced quite a bit of this raucous environment and didn't pay it much mind, but an encounter with a known New York gangster got his attention. Frankie Foster was waiting in Armstrong's dressing room when he finished a set one night. When Armstrong entered, Foster pulled out a large pistol and told Armstrong he was going to go back to New York and open at Connie's Inn. The club was struggling to stay open, while Armstrong's popularity continued to soar. Shocked by the firearm, Armstrong agreed, and once Foster left, he fretted over what to do.

Foster and the rest of the New York gang were expecting Armstrong to arrive the following morning, but Collins got him out of Chicago within hours of the encounter. Collins sent the band on a grueling series of gigs. They traveled across Illinois, Ohio, Kentucky, and West Virginia, followed incessantly by the mob. After weeks of touring, the band took a weeklong gig in Detroit's Graystone Ballroom. Once that was done, the band traveled to Wisconsin and Minnesota. While on the road, they saw some of the heartbreaking conditions created by the Great Depression, but they ended the tour on a high note when Armstrong returned to his home city in 1931.

In early June, Armstrong's train pulled into the station on Canal Street and was greeted by eight bands stretched across the railroad tracks. The procession that led him down Canal Street included his sister and many old friends. The following morning, Armstrong visited the Waif's Home and his mentor Peter Davis. Armstrong and his band were slated to be the first black musicians to play the Suburban Gardens. The Gardens had their own radio program, which had only ever broadcast white performers. The club was packed inside and out. Around ten thousand black New Orleanians awaited the star outside the building, unable to gain entrance on account of their race. When it came time for the announcer to introduce Armstrong and the band, he refused, claiming he couldn't announce him. Armstong took the opportunity to introduce the show himself.

Armstrong's return to New Orleans was marked by his generosity. He loved his city and gave his money freely. He handed bills to fans on the street and donated radios to inmates at the Waif's Home. He even sponsored a local baseball team that renamed itself Armstrong's Secret Nine.

In August, Lil came to visit him in New Orleans. While there, they agreed to a legal separation, though Lil continued to bill herself as Lil Hardin Armstrong when she played. The two stayed married, though they remained estranged from one another.

In September, the band went on a tour of the South, playing Dallas, Texas, traveling through Oklahoma, and then back to Dallas. They encountered racist police in Memphis and were locked up after a dispute over the size of their tour bus. Armstrong and his band were released after agreeing to play a benefit show. The show was broadcast over the radio, and Louis Armstrong acknowledged the Memphis police, who impeded their tour. "Ladies and gentlemen, I'm now going to dedicate this tune to the Memphis Police Force," Armstrong said before launching into the song "I'll Be Glad When You're Dead, You Rascal, You." Perhaps ironically, the local police were not offended but overjoyed at having a song dedicated to them.

After their release, the constant touring continued and the band crisscrossed the country, playing in cities like Boston, Philadelphia, Jersey City, New Haven, Baltimore, and Washington, DC. Rockwell accused Armstrong of breach of contract for not returning to Connie's Inn, at which point Armstrong countersued him.

While in New York, he appeared in two films. One was a Betty Boop cartoon. Armstrong appears as a floating head in the animated sky, singing as he pursues two characters. The other film, *A Rhapsody in Black and Blue*, featured him as a trumpeter playing in jazz heaven.

From November until March 1932, Armstrong recorded several songs in Chicago. These tunes included "Lazy River," "Star Dust," and "Georgia on my Mind." His band broke up after playing a few shows there. Armstrong went to California and played at the New Cotton Club once again, but stress from his legal troubles, fear of the mob, and money problems spurred him to seek a more distant escape. On July 9, Armstrong boarded the SS *Majestic* along with Collins, Collins's wife, and Alpha Smith. The SS *Majestic* was headed from New York to London, where Armstrong would kick off a European tour.

Upon arrival, Percy Mathison Brooks, the editor of music magazine *Melody Maker*, greeted Armstrong. According to Armstrong, Brooks addressed him as "Satchmo," an abbreviation of "Satchel Mouth," one of Armstrong's many nicknames. He got a kick out of the nickname, and it began to follow him. Armstrong played the London Palladium to a packed crowd. His English fans included William Walton, an up-and-coming composer, and William Primrose, a viola player. Not all reviews of Armstrong's material were positive, but his performances did garner a lot of attention.

Despite this success, he continued to have money troubles, much of which concerned his increasingly erratic manager. Collins would demand to be paid up front in cash before Armstrong went on and would become aggressive with venue owners. His drunken, unstable behavior concerned those close to Armstrong. Louis, however, knew the importance of having a white manager. Collins could help in his troubles with mob-connected Tommy Rockwell and Dutch Schultz. Without him, he was left with few options. Though Armstrong did not trust Collins entirely, he continued their professional relationship.

Armstrong would return to New York in November 1932 and get right back out on the road. Before long, it seemed years of strenuous playing had taken their toll. At a New Year's party in

Baltimore in 1933, Armstrong split his lip. He tried to lick the blood away, but without success. Eventually, he was forced to break from playing the rest of the night. However, he did not let this stop him from playing altogether. He went back to Chicago and played gigs there and in other Midwestern cities, but was back in Europe in the summer of 1933. He toured extensively, though his relationship with Collins continued to unravel.

For years, Armstrong had relied on Collins to look after his finances, bills, and paychecks, and by this point Armstrong considered his manager more like his employer. However, he found out while in London that Collins had not been entirely honest with Armstrong and had in fact caused the musician to accumulate a lot of debt. Furious but unable to get Collins's name off contracts for London's engagements, Armstrong stuck with him until September, when the contracts ended. Then, Collins left the country, but he took Armstrong's passport with him. Despite this, Armstrong continued his trek across Europe and played to huge crowds in Copenhagen and Stockholm, then went to Norway, the Netherlands, and back to England.

The next time Armstrong heard from Collins was in 1934, when he received a telegram from New York. The correspondence included a list of gigs Collins had lined up for Louis when he returned. Armstrong threw the message away immediately. He had no intention of mending their relationship. Collins would have no more part in Armstrong's career.

Armstrong spent most of 1934 resting. He saw the sights of London with Alpha Smith and later went to Paris, where they

Louis Armstrong gives a performance at the Paramount Theater in May 1937.

mingled with other celebrity expatriates of the time, such as fellow trumpeter Arthur Briggs and entertainer Josephine Baker.

In November 1934, he resumed playing gigs and recording. "On the Sunny Side of the Street" and "Song of the Vipers" were two songs he took to the studio. He also had his Paris debut at Salle Pleyel, to enthusiastic crowds. While he had offers to tour the country, Armstrong declined and made his way back to America. Collins was threatening to sue, and Lil was already suing him for six thousand dollars, as she believed she was owed monies for songs they had collaborated on together. The condition of his split lip also demanded that he rest. He lay up in Chicago nursing his lip and other wounds until May 1935, when he approached a man who he believed could solve all his problems: Joe Glaser.

6 The Impact of Louis Armstrong

"I never did want to be a mucky muck star."

Louis Armstrong

Louis Armstrong spent his life defining jazz music's precepts and steadfastly pushing himself to develop his sound. No modern jazz artist plays without taking some cue from Armstrong's **repertoire**. Even artists who played during his lifetime paid Louis their respects and acknowledged him as the musician who lit the way for jazz. His frenetic horn playing electrified the burgeoning art form; his high notes dazzled listeners and fellow musicians alike. Not only did Armstrong mold jazz music with his cornet and trumpet playing, but he also revolutionized American singing with his instantly recognizable gravelly croon.

Opposite: Armstrong listens to his manager, Joe Glaser, after a concert.

From playing the streets of New Orleans to recording for OKeh, to electrifying the black and tan scene in New York City and ruling the big band scene in the 1940s, Armstrong became a prominent and influential figure in American history. He happily devoted his entire life to his craft. In fact, he has the distinction of being the oldest artist to have a number-one record with his rendition of "Hello Dolly!," which topped the charts when he was sixty-three years old.

Although Armstrong only had a fifth-grade education, he was an avid writer. After moving from New Orleans to Chicago to join his mentor Joe Oliver, Armstrong bought his first typewriter and began to compose letters home. He soon found that he loved writing ("typing," as he called it) and continued to compose letters and autobiographical narratives for the rest of his life. His writings have helped to form a complex, rich picture of his life and the evolution of jazz music. He published *Swing That Music* in 1936 and became the first jazz musician to publish a memoir. The book was also the first widely read memoir by a black American. Though he was a victim of racism throughout his life, his humor and writings helped to humanize blackness. Armstrong was not outspoken about race relations during his lifetime, but he did manage to break down barriers. For instance, he was the first black musician to stipulate in his contract that he would not play a hotel that he could not also stay at, the first African American entertainer to host a nationally sponsored radio program, and the first black actor to earn top billing in a major motion picture.

While white Americans struggled with how to appropriately interact with black American culture and people, Armstrong was just interested in making music. He did his best to avoid talking about anything he deemed to be too political—understandable considering he grew up under harsh segregation, violence, and extreme poverty. Still, Armstrong didn't care who was playing an instrument; if it sounded good, he wanted to play with them. This desire to connect with fellow musicians led him to form one of jazz's first deep friendships across the color line.

Bix Beiderbecke was a white teenager from Davenport, Iowa, who loved jazz music. He would often go down to the riverfront to hear the sounds of trumpets from the excursion dance boats that floated down the Mississippi. It was here that Beiderbecke is believed to have first met Louis Armstrong.

In the summer of 1920, the SS *Capitol* pulled in to dock at Davenport, and Beiderbecke stood on the dock, mesmerized by Armstrong's cornet playing. From that moment on, Beiderbecke became inspired. He taught himself cornet, and the two met again years later when they were both headlining clubs in Chicago. Beiderbecke was all over the north side of Chicago, but Armstrong was the rage on the south side. Don Cheatham, a jazz trumpeter, remembered the Chicago music scene back then, saying, "Everything was Bix Beiderbecke back then. But on the South Side, there was Louis Armstrong, who brought out so many beautiful records that he overpowered everybody."

Social life was strictly segregated at the time, and black musicians could not play alongside white musicians onstage. However, the two did support each other and jammed together privately. Saxophonist Bud Freeman remembered their relationship, saying, "Louis loved Bix and Bix loved Louis, of course. Whenever Bix would come to town and go down to hear Louis Armstrong at the Sunset, we'd find out about it and go down there and sit at a table with Bix."

Armstrong and Beiderbecke would meet at Lincoln Gardens and play "Dippermouth Blues" together while they were both still playing Chicago. Around 1924, the two were both making their debuts in New York City. Armstrong was playing with Fletcher Henderson's orchestra at the Roseland, while Bix played with the Wolverines at the Cinderella Ballroom. The two continued to support each other musically, and in July 1928, Armstrong saw Bix perform as a star soloist in Paul Whiteman's orchestra in Chicago. He was astonished at Beiderbecke's sound and praised his solo: "All of a sudden Bix stood up and took a solo and those pretty notes went right through me. You take a man with a pure tone like Bix and no matter how loud the other fellas in the band may be blowing, that pure tone will cut through it all."

Ultimately, Bix Beiderbecke would come to a bad end. He struggled with alcoholism throughout his short life and died before the age of thirty from pneumonia. Still, his music lived on. Though his style of playing is distinct from Louis Armstrong's, Armstrong was one of his greatest inspirations.

Bix Beiderbecke shared Armstrong's love for jazz music. The two often played music together privately.

While Beiderbecke was taken with Armstrong's skills on the cornet and trumpet, another white music lover would soon be inspired by Armstrong's singing style. Bing Crosby had just signed with Paul Whiteman's orchestra when he first saw Armstrong perform in New York. He was transfixed, and like many other singers, he began to imitate Armstrong's scat style after hearing his recording of "Heebie Jeebies." Crosby and Armstrong were both involved in the Los Angeles jazz scene in the early 1930s and struck up a friendship. Both artists played gigs that were also broadcast to radio audiences. Armstrong remembered his years playing on the same airwaves as Crosby fondly, saying:

> *Every night between their outfit and our outfit, we used to burn up the air, every night ... Bing and Gus Arnheim & Co. would broadcast first every night and leave the ether wave sizzling hot. Just right for us when we would burst on in there from the Cotton Club. Oh, it was lots of fun. The same listeners would catch both programs before going to bed.*

The two didn't just complement each other on the air; Crosby was heavily influenced by Armstrong's singing and imitated his style to great success. During this time, Armstrong also experimented with crooning, an intimate style of singing that lent itself to ballads. In the 1930s, both performers began to appear in films. In 1936, Crosby was slated to appear in *Pennies from Heaven.*

However, he demanded that Armstrong be cast in the film. Not only did Armstrong appear, but he received top billing, and his image was featured on posters and advertisements promoting the film. His star power steadily rose, and he appeared in seven more films. In February 1960, Louis Armstrong received a star on the Hollywood Walk of Fame, a coveted honor for American film actors.

In addition to acting together, Crosby and Armstrong appeared on the NBC radio show *Kraft Music Hall* from the mid 1930s into the 1940s. Crosby would often host and have Armstrong on as a guest. Their entertaining joint and solo appearances on radio, in films, and eventually on television offered a glimpse into the personalities of the stars of early popular music. From scat singing to crooning ballads, Crosby and Armstrong's influence set the standards for American jazz singing. The two also collaborated on *Bing & Satchmo*, a studio album recorded in 1960. Crosby himself acknowledged Armstrong's essential position among American performers, saying, "American music begins and ends with Louis Armstrong."

Various conductors and performers echoed Crosby's praise of Armstrong throughout the years. Eddie Condon, a Chicago jazz musician and critic, was one of many enthralled by Armstrong during his first days in Chicago. Condon remembered seeing Oliver and Armstrong playing at Lincoln Gardens:

> *As the door opened the trumpets, King and Louis—one or both—soared above everything else. The*

whole joint was rocking. Tables, chairs, walls, people moved with the rhythm. It was hypnosis at first hearing. Armstrong seemed able to hear what Oliver was improvising and reproduce it himself at the same time. Then the two wove around each other like suspicious women talking about the same man.

Another unknown patron observed there was so much music in the air that if you held up a horn it would play by itself.

When Armstrong began playing in New York, Fletcher Henderson is said to have instructed new members of his band to play like Louis. Likewise, Duke Ellington is credited with saying he wanted Louis Armstrong on every instrument. Musicians everywhere imitated the jumping syncopation of Armstrong's infectious trumpet playing, just as singers would model his low, gravelly croon. Armstrong remained notably humble despite his influence on the music world, though he did acknowledge his gift. He valued his creative partnerships and sang the praises of his most significant mentors until his dying day.

Upon reflection on his days playing at Lincoln Gardens with Joe Oliver, Armstrong credits their deep relationship with allowing interplay between their instruments, something that other musicians could not match:

The word just spread around, Joe Oliver got a little second cornet player and they're making breaks

> *together and doing a lot of things together, you got to hear them. I was interested in Joe Oliver. I loved the way he played and I practically knew everything he played so I put notes to it, surprised him, I could make duets to whatever … all the musicians thought that was great. They tried it and everything but they didn't concentrate like we did, couldn't do it. Unless they wrote it down but we didn't write anything—never did write it down.*

Duke Ellington, a classically trained musician and bandleader from Washington, DC, rose to fame at the same time as Armstrong. The two often played together on the road. In fact, when Armstrong and his band made their way to New York, they initially found work playing a gig that Ellington's band had to cancel at the last minute. They recorded *Louis Armstrong and Duke Ellington: The Great Summit/Complete Sessions* in 1961. At that point, both musicians were jazz icons, and the sophisticated recording reflects their prowess.

Armstrong had another notable partnership with singer Ella Fitzgerald. In the 1950s, Armstrong crept into his fourth decade of performing but was still captivating audiences, as was Fitzgerald, who was heralded as "The First Lady of Song." The two collaborated on three albums together: *Ella and Louis*, *Ella and Louis Again*, and *Porgy and Bess*, which was inducted

Louis Armstrong (*left*) and Ella Fitzgerald (*right*) sing at the Empire Room of the Waldorf Astoria in New York City on March 30, 1971.

into the Grammy Hall of Fame in 2001. These recordings were incredibly popular, and in 1997, *The Complete Ella Fitzgerald & Louis Armstrong on Verve* was released. Recorded collaborations between the two are still popular with fans today. The two also played shows together in 1956 at the Hollywood Bowl. Tracks recorded at this performance would later be included as bonus material for an album released more than forty years later.

While fellow musicians were fond of acknowledging Armstrong's achievements, he also received recognition from fans and professional music organizations. He reigned as King Zulu during the 1949 Mardi Gras celebrations in New Orleans and graced the covers of *Time* and *Life* magazines. His Hot Five and Hot Seven recordings are essential listening for any jazz enthusiast, and his singing introduced scat singing to a national audience. According to *Billboard*, he had nineteen Top Ten records. Armstrong even managed to steal the top spot on the chart from the Beatles in 1964. The last song that became a hit in his lifetime was first appreciated not in America but in London. "What A Wonderful World" sat atop the British charts for a month in 1968, but the song wasn't acknowledged stateside until its use in the 1987 film *Good Morning, Vietnam*. He was awarded a Grammy for Best Male Vocal Performance after being nominated for "Hello, Dolly!" in 1965. The Academy of Recording Arts and Sciences posthumously awarded him with a Grammy Lifetime Achievement Award in 1972, and several of his recordings have been inducted into the Grammy Hall of Fame.

Louis Armstrong was able to have a hand in defining American music because he rose to prominence at a time when America was going through dramatic transition. He was one of thousands of African Americans who participated in the Great Migration and moved from the South to northern cities in search of greater opportunity. His participation in this social movement allowed him to make music that resonated with others who found themselves far from home. He went to New York, a city with a higher black population than any other northern city, and played nightly in Harlem, the home of the National Association for the Advancement of Colored People (NAACP), Zora Neale Hurston, Langston Hughes and W. E. B. Dubois. Armstrong's music will forever be associated with the Harlem Renaissance, as his innovative playing served as a soundtrack for a moment in history when African Americans were defining what it meant to be both black and American. Armstrong's success onstage and in Hollywood paved the way for other black performers to achieve international fame. He endured humiliating racism throughout his career but faced each instance with a grace and professionalism that helped lay the foundation for the burgeoning civil rights movement.

Armstrong didn't just establish the tenets and future of jazz; he gave jazz its language. His fans imitated his speech and his dress; performers used large white handkerchiefs in honor of the ones he mopped his brow with onstage. He was the first person to be recorded referring to people as "cats," and those who heard him speak ate up his colorful **lexicon**. Louis Armstrong is one

This graffitti artwork memorializes Louis Armstrong.

of America's first musical icons, and as a result, it is sometimes difficult to say when Armstrong's work is influencing a musician. His rhythmic improvisation taught the country how to swing, and the 4/4 tempo—the standard of jazz—was introduced by Armstrong. From his style to his unique phrasing to the way he structured his songs, American musicians of every stripe imitated Armstrong, to the point that his work essentially established the tenets of American music.

7 Challenges and Controversy

"He was born poor, died rich, and never hurt anyone on the way."

Duke Ellington on Louis Armstrong

Throughout his life, Louis Armstrong faced many challenges. First, he rose to fame at a time when jazz was in its infancy. It was difficult to make a name for himself, but his talent brought him the fame he so rightly deserved. He lived through the Great Migration, the Harlem Renaissance, and the Great Depression, and injected his rhythm and blues and signature timing into the jazz genre, changing it forever. While the country transitioned racially and economically, Armstrong faced challenges in his personal life as well. During Armstrong's

Opposite: Armstrong's early career developed during the Prohibition era. Here, an FBI officer breaks open barrels of confiscated alcohol, circa 1924.

early life in New Orleans, he witnessed prostitution, gambling, and violence. He ran the streets as a child and was an inmate at the Colored Waif's Home for a time. As a teenager, he worked in rough clubs and dance halls.

Becoming a professional saw Armstrong face more obstacles. He rose to fame during **Prohibition**, often playing in secret clubs that served alcohol and hosted gangsters. While he managed to avoid physical violence, he was under threat by the Mafia for years. Eventually he was plagued by lawsuits and breach-of-contract disagreements, and while he did not die poor, he made much less money over his lifetime than he could have, due to his lack of royalties received for some of his most popular recordings. Straightening out his legal issues and conflicts with the Mafia was also expensive, though Armstrong was glad to pay for peace of mind at that point in his career.

Louis Armstrong also bore the burden of harsh racism throughout his life. He grew up during a time when public life was segregated by skin color, and at times, he was forced to navigate situations where he was expected to play for white audiences but not speak to them. Reviews of his early performances are filled with racist stereotypes; his performances overseas were similarly critiqued. Armstrong smiled through all of this and made his music his focus despite hateful rhetoric and situations.

Armstrong had trouble with the law as a young artist as well. He smoked marijuana throughout his life and believed it had medicinal properties. However, this habit also got him into trouble and saw him arrested on several occasions. Still, he was able to avoid serving any hard time.

Armstrong had run-ins with racist police officers when he toured the southern United States and even boycotted his home city after New Orleans outlawed integrated bands in the mid-1950s. In fact, he preferred to play overseas because while he still experienced racism, he worried less about the threat of violence.

Armstrong prided himself on putting his music first, and as a result, his relationships often suffered. He was married four times and had multiple girlfriends throughout his life. His marriage to his first wife, Daisy, was violent, one that Armstrong ended only after meeting his second wife, Lil Hardin. Hardin was integral to Armstrong's career. She pushed him to seek top billing and encouraged him to lead his own bands. Though they divorced in 1938, Hardin continued to use Armstrong's name and is undoubtedly the reason that Armstrong was able to attain celebrity status. Alpha Smith was Armstrong's girlfriend for years before he finally divorced Lil and made Alpha his third wife. She became preoccupied with Louis's money, and they divorced in order for Armstrong to marry his fourth and final wife, Lucille Wilson. Lucille was a dancer he had seen performing at the Cotton Club. The two found a way to live together peacefully, though they didn't always agree. Armstrong continued to see other women, which strained their union, but Wilson supported Armstrong into his later years despite her husband's infidelity.

He wrote about what he thought made his marriage to Wilson successful later in life:

> *She's just a fine human being who knows what it takes to relax me and make me feel good. The women who marry me must respect my program and way of life. Lucille has done such a swell job of being my wife that I doubt I'll ever want to replace her with another. She's almost an ideal type of woman to me. We get along real well and as I have said before, understand each other. We can stay at home for hours and days without any friction. She doesn't bother me until I want to be bothered.*

In addition to personal challenges, Armstrong also wrestled with artistic struggles. One aspect of performing Armstrong always wanted to do was sing. However, Joe Oliver and Fletcher Henderson rarely allowed it. Despite singing in the Broadway show *Hot Chocolates*, his flair for brass saw him **pigeonholed** as a trumpet player.

Armstrong also struggled with health issues that impacted his playing. His lips began to harden and bleed in the mid 1930s after years of stressing them during rehearsals and performances. His injuries would demand that he rest for months, though he never completely recovered. Eventually, he would take to using creams and salves to ease his irritated mouth.

Armstrong shares a kiss with his fourth wife, Lucille Wilson.

Throughout his life, Armstrong maintained a happy-go-lucky disposition, though a troubled personal life sometimes lay behind his disarming smile. Louis Armstrong gave a multitude of interviews throughout his career but also left his own take on the events of his life through his writing. Armstrong documented his life extensively from the 1920s until his death in 1971. He expressed himself in writing with the same unique exuberance he used in speech, and his typewritten work is filled with stresses all his own. His memoirs, letters, and other writings allow readers to better understand Armstrong's life and challenges, as well as the story of the evolution of music and celebrity in America.

He was born to May Ann, a teenage mother who sometimes earned money through prostitution. Though May Ann's activities added to the instability in little Louis's life, he loved her fiercely. He later wrote about struggling to get by as a child and credited her with giving him the most important life lesson:

> *I had to work and help May Ann, - put bread on the table, since it was just the three of us living in this one big room, which was all that we could afford. But we were happy. My mother had one thing that no matter how much schooling anyone has—and that was Good Common Sense (and respect for human beings). Yea. That's My Diploma—All through my life I remembered it.*

Growing up in the poorest, most violent district in the city exposed Armstrong to violence and sexuality at a young age, but he loved his city and saw the beauty in the most desperate of circumstances.

While delivering coal for the Karnofsky family, he saw the most criminal elements of his environment. Armstrong reflected on his childhood's rough environment in writing during a hospitalization at New York's Beth Israel Hospital toward the end of his life.

> *When I helped Alex Karnofsky on the wagon, we used to run across a lot of bottles. They came from either by Drunks or a fight. Maybe two women—fighting over the same pimp. It was quite a few pimps who had Stables. And their chicks used to fight like mad. A Stable means that one pimp has several girls in one house, hustling for him.*
>
> *Another thing which caused a lot of trouble, even killing scrapes—where the same whore will have two Suckers' giving her their money at the same time … it could turn out to be an awful Killing Scrape, and most time it did. Or a hell of a fist fight or a cutting scrape, with knives, razors, etc.*

Armstrong was not a violent child despite his surroundings, but he did get into trouble with the law. Eventually, he was sent to the Waif's Home, where he got his first taste of formal musical education. While there, he became skilled enough to be offered a position playing cornet on a steamboat on the Mississippi River. This opportunity gave him the chance to develop musically and to escape his first wife, Daisy.

One relationship that gave Armstrong great joy throughout his life was with a child for whom he took responsibility when he was just a teenager. In 1915, Armstrong's cousin Flora Myles gave birth to a baby boy named Clarence. When he first saw the child, Armstrong remarked, "There I saw the baby Clarence, and it took all the gloom out of me."

The child's father was an older white man living in the neighborhood who had raped Flora. Because of racial codes at the time, Flora's family was not able to seek justice from the courts. Instead of seeking revenge, Armstrong decided to make Clarence his responsibility: "There wasn't anyone in the family who could take care of him properly. I just could do it myself." Armstrong made Clarence's well-being a priority, and the two got along famously. "I had a little ol' beat up job wasn't paying much, but the kid liked me so much—and I was crazy about him, too—I used to take him every place I went," Armstrong later recorded.

As Clarence thrived, although with mental disabilities, his mother deteriorated. She never regained her strength after giving birth, but she saw how well Armstrong cared for her son. Before dying, Flora gave Clarence the last name of Armstrong, making it clear that she wanted Louis to act as Clarence's sole permanent guardian.

When Armstrong left New Orleans for Chicago, Clarence stayed behind. However, after his wedding to Lil Hardin, Armstrong sent for the boy. "I had the folks down in New Orleans whom I left Clarence to live with when I went to Chicago put a tag on Clarence, put him on a train, and send him to me. It was one swell, grand reunion," Louis wrote. His relationship with Clarence was a source of great pride, especially in light of his estranged relationship with his own father.

Armstrong made sure the boy felt at home in his new city. He gave Clarence his own room and found a school that specialized in teaching mentally disabled children. Louis would later write about how happy Clarence was: "He turned out to be one of the best baseball, basketball, and football players in the whole school. And everybody knew him and called him Little Louis Armstrong."

Years later, when he returned to Chicago from New York, Armstrong would move Clarence. He and Clarence began to spend time at the home of his girlfriend Alpha Smith and Smith's mother. Both women loved Clarence, and it was decided that he would move in with them.

As years progressed, Armstrong continued to work at clubs and on movie sets across the United States and overseas. Clarence sometimes visited Armstrong on tour and spent time with him in his dressing room before and after performances. Upon Armstrong's death, Clarence received five thousand dollars. Despite their strong parent-child bond, Armstrong had never legally adopted Clarence, and he lived out the rest of his life in obscurity.

In addition to Armstrong's struggles with family relationships, he also ran into trouble with his managers and, in turn, the mob. After leaving Lil's group at Dreamland Café, Armstrong began playing at the Sunset Café for Joe Glaser, a known associate of legendary Al Capone, who often came into the Sunset to see Louis's shows. Federal agents raided the Sunset Café regularly.

Joe Glaser would later rescue Armstrong from debts and mob conflicts as his manager later in life.

During Armstrong's second visit to New York City, Tommy Rockwell managed him. Rockwell got him the gig at Connie's Inn and subsequently helped him secure his role in *Hot Chocolates* and gigs at a variety of clubs in Harlem. Connie's Inn was teeming with gangsters, and one of Armstrong's biggest fans was co-owner and murderer Dutch Schultz. This admiration would pose problems for Armstrong when he left New York shortly after the stock market crashed and went to California to play in Culver City. Around this time, Johnny Collins had become his manager. Armstrong was led to believe that he and Tommy Rockwell had some agreement, but Rockwell and Dutch Schultz were furious when word got out that someone else was managing Armstrong.

Johnny Collins stepped in to manage Louis while he was playing in Culver City. Initially, Armstrong was under the impression that Collins had some arrangement with Rockwell, but as he began to receive threats from the mob regarding his gigs, he realized that the two managers were not affiliated. Collins was not only dishonest but also an alcoholic who would go on drunken rampages, during which he disparaged Louis. He would demand venues pay him up front and in cash before Armstrong played.

In 1934, after Collins left Armstrong stranded without a passport overseas, he went through a series of interim managers. First, he was connected to Englishman Jack Hylton, who wanted him to play with a rising saxophone star named Coleman Hawkins, but Louis refused to appear and perform. His relationship with Hylton ended, and he signed with Audrey Thacker, another English manager. Despite Thacker's wishes, Armstrong did not resume a full touring schedule. He moved through England and Paris, playing when he wanted and mixing with other celebrity expatriates, such as Josephine Baker, Bobby Jones, and Arthur Briggs.

Even still, during his career, Armstrong became a legend, especially abroad. In October 1934, Armstrong recorded "Song of the Vipers," a song that celebrated jazz and marijuana. The record was pulled from shelves in America after the song's references were made clear, but its popularity in Europe fueled Armstrong's fame. In November, he performed at the Salle Rameau in Paris to a rapturous crowd. Armstrong's growing popularity attracted the French promoter N.J. Canetti, who sent Armstrong to tour London, Belgium, France, Italy, and Switzerland. With the frenetic touring schedule and long hours of playing, Armstrong's lip issues were eventually aggravated. He was forced to cancel a number of performances, which angered Canetti. The French promoter canceled all of Armstrong's remaining tour dates and accused Armstrong of faking his injuries in order to avoid sharing the stage with his talented pianist, Herman Chittison.

Armstrong returned to America in late January 1935, where he rested in Chicago and allowed his split lip to heal. When Armstrong was feeling better, he emerged from his hideaway and sought out Joe Glaser to help him with his money, mob, and legal troubles.

He was facing a breach-of-contract suit from Canetti in France, and in England, Thacker was demanding that he honor a yearlong contract. He begged Joe Glaser to help him straighten out his affairs. Glaser was struggling as well, but the two paired up under a casual but mutually beneficial arrangement. When Glaser protested that he was too broke to act as Armstrong's manager, Armstrong told him, "That doesn't make any difference. You collect the money. You pay me one thousand dollars every week free and clear. You pay my band, the travel and the hotel expenses, my income tax, and you take everything that's left."

Glaser set about solving Armstrong's problems one by one. He arranged interviews and performances. He paid Collins $5,000 for Armstrong's contract. Glaser had a prior relationship with Tommy Rockwell and was able to keep him away from Armstrong. Glaser opted not to send Armstrong on overseas tours as a way of avoiding the promoters he had upset in Europe. Once he had more or less settled Armstrong's affairs, they went on tour together, and Glaser learned the business of managing a musician performance by performance. When Louis Armstrong died, he was worth around $530,700 while Joe Glaser, who died just two years earlier, was worth more than $3 million. Despite appearances, Armstrong swore by his beloved manager all his life, and his wife Lucille also vouched for Glaser.

One of Armstrong's chief struggles throughout his career was with racism. The United States practiced social segregation for the great majority of his career, and this meant that he had to play twice as many performances, often in separate locations, in order to reach the same number of fans. While some have criticized Armstrong for not speaking out enough against racism, they have to consider the conditions under which Armstrong was attempting to make a living. He would only make enough to make ends meet if he played for white audiences, and those white audiences were interested in seeing racist material that demeaned black people and affirmed their sense of superiority. Armstrong was still able to invest his performances with humanity and grace. In 1957, he spoke out harshly against Dwight D. Eisenhower for not interfering with violence in Arkansas that occurred when nine African American students attempted to integrate a white high school. Armstrong also refused to attend the Oscars shortly after Martin Luther King Jr.'s murder. Touring the South posed considerable issues, and Armstrong would insist Joe Glaser be on the bus so that the band could have a white man onboard to vouch for them. Despite his struggles with racism, Armstrong inspired many African Americans to pursue their dreams even in the face of hate.

Louis Armstrong had his share of challenges throughout his professional life. From an unstable, erratic home life to a series of unfaithful marriages, Louis Armstrong's personal life was also trying at times. Though he spent time incarcerated, was threatened by the mob, faced several legal disputes, and struggled to find the right manager, Louis Armstrong was able to showcase his incredible trumpet playing and singing skills while building his fan base. He ultimately reached international superstardom and changed the course of music forever.

ensational melody! Bing Crosby and Louis Armstrong and his band render "Now You Has J

A SOL C. SIEGEL PRODUCTION

-G-M esents "HIGH SOCIETY" in VISTAVIS Color by TECHNICO

COUNTRY OF ORIGIN U. S. A.

4

8 The King of Jazz

"Armstrong is to music what Einstein is to physics and the Wright Brothers are to travel."

Jazz documentary producer Ken Burns

When Louis Armstrong returned to Chicago in 1935, he was exhausted. He had been touring regularly for nearly fifteen years, his lip was raw, and he had to use salves to try and heal the split. Johnny Collins had deserted him overseas months ago. His lip injuries, dwindling finances, and legal troubles plagued him. He rested until May and returned to performing with a man he had handpicked: Joe Glaser.

Opposite: Promotional material for the 1956 movie *High Society*, starring Louis Armstrong (*right*) and Bing Crosby (*left*).

Joe Glaser was not a successful talent manager. When Armstrong propositioned him, he was also wrestling with trouble with the law as a result of his mob activities and his work as a pimp. In fact, Glaser faced a variety of criminal charges before partnering with Armstrong and was just as desperate as his new trumpeter client. Armstrong adored Glaser and believed him to be the answer to his many problems. When Glaser protested that he could not become his manager because he himself was broke, Armstrong ignored him. He suggested Glaser make payment arrangements for his travel and lodging, pay his band and income taxes, give him one thousand dollars a week, and keep the rest.

Armstrong's offer was too good for Glaser to pass up. He set about clearing up Armstrong's debts. He paid Collins off for Armstrong's "contract" and knew Rockwell as a result of earlier business contacts. Glaser made sure that Rockwell and Armstrong never crossed paths and dealt with Armstrong's complaints from overseas in a similar fashion: he simply decided to keep Louis stateside. Glaser immediately set up a series of one-night performances and an interview with a Chicago jazz publication that announced his official return to the stage. Glaser also managed to settle recording disputes with Columbia and Victor records and negotiated Louis a contract with Decca Records. Armstrong was recording songs by October and would continue to make music with Decca for the next seven years. His first Decca songs included "I'm in the Mood for Love," "You Are My Lucky Star," "La Cucaracha," and "Got a Bran' New Suit." Louis sang on all four recordings. He would later record "When the Saints Go Marching In" for Decca in 1938. It would become a jazz standard. Armstrong reunited with Glaser to great benefit for both parties. In October 1935, Armstrong and his new band opened at Connie's Inn and played there for four months. Armstrong's return could not have been more perfectly timed, as the country was on the cusp of being swept by the swing music phenomenon.

The next few years flew by for Armstrong as Glaser had him on tour most of the time. Armstrong and his new band traveled the country, hitting as many major cities as possible as often as they could. Glaser always traveled with the band when their tour took them into the South. A white man was necessary for obtaining food while traveling, as many establishments refused to serve black people. There was also the threat of physical violence; Glaser's presence meant that a white man would be available to speak for them if they ran into trouble.

In addition to getting Armstrong out on the road, Glaser set about making Louis a film star. Armstrong had started making movies in 1930 with *Ex-Flame*. In 1936, he appeared as a traveling musician who converts a haunted house into a nightclub in the film *Pennies from Heaven*. Hollywood films that featured African American actors at this time tended to perpetuate the most harmful of stereotypes. The material Louis had to work with as an actor served to underline the inferiority of blacks to whites, and Armstrong's reviews were generally racist. Nevertheless, Armstrong's work on *Pennies from Heaven* opened the door to future possibilities in Hollywood. This role made Armstrong the first African American to earn top billing in a major motion picture, no small feat in 1936. The film's title song also became one of Armstrong's biggest hits. The same year he published *Swing That Music*, a memoir that made use of the letters and other writings Armstrong had been doing since he left New Orleans. Armstrong's influence on the art form makes his work required reading for any jazz fan as it gives a behind-the-scenes look at the development of jazz's distinct sound.

Armstrong appeared in *Artists and Models* in 1937. The comedy featured a racy song-and-dance routine between Louis and Martha Raye, a white actress. The film drew widespread criticism for its portrayal of interracial sexuality. Elected officials in Atlanta, Georgia, banded together to condemn the film. The editor of a major Louisiana newspaper wrote the following criticism of the movie:

> *For negroes and whites to be shown in social equity is offensive in this part of the country, where the races have nothing socially in common … there is a color line, and it will always be drawn.*

Armstrong's predicament meant that he could appear in films with white actors, but audiences would not be receptive to his interacting with white actors. As a result, his roles served to underline racial stereotypes and inequalities. He often appeared as a jazz musician and performed separate from white people.

Armstrong performs "Jeepers Creepers" in the 1938 movie *Going Places.*

While no one could blame Louis Armstrong for finding the balancing act that racial codes demanded in the 1930s too much to navigate, he earned an Academy Award nomination the very next year. In 1938's *Going Places*, Armstrong transcended another racist role when he appeared as a stableman referred to as "Uncle Tom." Armstrong's scene in which he sang to a wild horse earned critical acclaim. "Jeepers Creepers" became a hit song in addition to earning him a key position among the few black actors working in Hollywood. Despite the limiting roles he received, Louis Armstrong was proud of his work as an actor and became a founding member of the Negro Actors Guild.

Armstrong wasn't just breaking barriers onscreen during this time. In April 1937, he hosted *The Fleischmann's Yeast Hour,* a musical variety radio program broadcast on CBS, in place of Rudy Vallee. Armstrong's appearance on the program marked the first time in American history that a black person hosted a national broadcast.

In between filming movies and radio programs, Armstrong was touring. During his travels through Savannah, Georgia, he ran into his destitute mentor, Joe Oliver. Oliver had chosen to remain in the South through the Great Depression and had wrestled with setback after setback. His tour bus often broke down and gum disease finally ravaged his mouth to the point where he could no longer play. He was peddling potatoes on the street when Armstrong crossed his path for the last time. Louis gave Oliver all the money he had on him and also took up a collection from his band members. Not long after, in April 1938, Oliver died.

Armstrong had a promising career by the end of the 1930s despite his struggles when the decade began; his personal life also saw significant changes. In September 1938, he divorced Lil Hardin. They had been legally married for fourteen years but had only truly lived as man and wife for two years. Armstrong had been seeing Alpha Smith for several years and made her his third wife that October. When that marriage ended, Louis would blame Alpha's attraction to his money for souring the relationship. However, Armstrong was never good at being a faithful husband. Shortly after he and Alpha married, he attended a performance at a new Cotton Club that had opened near Times Square and found himself taken with a young dancer named Lucille Wilson.

World War II began in 1939, and Armstrong continued to tour relentlessly. Swing music was the new rage among American youth, and Louis, who had helped define the wild new style of playing, was able to carve a niche for himself. He began to play shows for soldiers in gymnasiums instead of gangsters in nightclubs. At a show in Panama City, Florida, in 1941, soldiers even presented Armstrong with a medal shaped like crossed cannons in honor of his morale-boosting music. Military audiences were, of course, segregated, and Armstrong often performed back-to-back shows for white and black audiences.

In 1942, Armstrong and Alpha Smith divorced. Their separation was reported and debated in jazz publications, with Armstrong himself reaching out to one columnist to clarify his complaints about Smith's transgressions as his wife. If Armstrong was upset by the breakup, he did not take long to mourn the loss. That same year Armstrong married Lucille Wilson, the beautiful dark-skinned dancer he had met years before. Armstrong went right back to touring after the wedding, ever a devotee to his philosophy of putting his horn first.

He continued to tour and visited Montana, Idaho, and Minnesota before pausing to film *Cabin in the Sky*. The film was an all-black musical about the struggle for a man's soul. Armstrong played one of Lucifer's henchmen and of course played trumpet during a big dance number. Many of Armstrong's scenes were cut from the final version of the film.

The early 1940s saw a resurgence of interest in early jazz music, and Armstrong toured incessantly, taking advantage of the renewed popularity. Lucille joined him on tour and found living out of a suitcase unsettling. In 1943, Lucille arranged to put a down payment on a house in Queens that Louis was apprehensive about living in. The road had been his home since he was a teenager, but he would grow to love returning to the house in Queens. The couple lived there until their deaths.

As World War II drew to a close in 1945, so did the country's fascination with big band swing. On May 7, 1947, Armstrong played a very successful jazz show at New York Town Hall. Months later, Glaser would organize a new group called Louis Armstrong and His All Stars. This six-piece band would see many changes in terms of its members, but Armstrong would continue to appear with the group throughout his career. Jazz legends like Earl Hines, Jack Teagarden, Barney Bigard, Trummy Young, Edmond Hall, Billy Kyle, and Tyree Glenn all played in Louis Armstrong and His All Stars.

While Armstrong was still able to make money touring and playing music, a new form of jazz was becoming popular: bebop. Fans of the new form claimed jazz as their own abstract expression and distanced themselves from Armstrong's foundational style. Armstrong was not shy about denouncing bebop, and for the first time in his life, he found that he was not at the helm determining the path of his chosen art form.

Armstrong kept touring and making films, but he was also in the recording studio. He kept working for Decca into the early 1950s. He recorded hits like "Blueberry Hill," "That Lucky Old Sun," "La Vie En Rose," "A Kiss to Build a Dream On" and "I Get Ideas." While bebop had cut into Armstrong's fan base, he ended the 1940s in true celebrity fashion. In 1949, he reigned as King Zulu at the Mardi Gras celebration and was also the first jazz musician to grace the front cover of *Time* magazine.

Armstrong spent much of the 1950s on the road, and when he wasn't touring he was making films or recording. Louis Armstrong and His All Stars would play an international tour at least once a year, and Armstrong saw his popularity overseas rise steadily. In

1952, he toured all over the globe. Armstrong went to Hawaii, Canada, Germany, Belgium, Switzerland, Scandinavia, Italy, and North Africa. A year later, he played himself in the Hollywood production *The Glen Miller Story* after a short tour with Benny Goodman, a swing bandleader and clarinetist. As 1953 drew to a close, Armstrong set out on his first tour of Japan. In 1954, Armstrong kept up his relentless pace with a tour of Australia, playing show after show to sold-out crowds of thousands of admiring fans. He also published his second book that year. This one covered his life until the year 1922 and was called *Satchmo: My Life In New Orleans.* Armstrong managed to get some studio time in as well, recording *Louis Armstrong Plays W.C. Handy* for Columbia Records.

The mid 1950s saw Armstrong continue his globetrotting. By now, he was regularly referred to by his nickname, Satchmo. He appeared in the United States playing cities like Los Angeles and his hometown New Orleans and international locales like Sweden, the Netherlands, and Italy. In 1955, he recorded the top ten hit record *Satch Plays Fats*, a compilation of Fats Waller songs. That year, he also recorded his own rendition of "Mack the Knife," a Kurt Weill song. The single would hold the number-one spot on the Australian charts for four weeks the following year. It also cracked the Top Forty in America. The media began to refer to Armstrong as "Ambassador Satch," on account of his soaring popularity overseas.

In 1956, Armstrong played himself in the film *High Society*, which starred Bing Crosby and Grace Kelly. He spent more time on set than he had on his previous films; he and his band worked for twenty-three days on the film. While reviewers were not entirely taken by the finished product, critics praised Armstrong's performance for bringing life to the picture. He collaborated with Ella Fitzgerald in the recording studio and visited the Gold Coast (modern-day Ghana) in May. There he played for an audience of more than one hundred thousand people in the capital, Accra. Journalist Edward R. Murrow made the trip as well, and footage from Armstrong's time in Africa was included in the documentary *Satchmo the Great*, released in 1957.

That same year, Armstrong found his voice in politics. Though he had tried to make the best of the circumstances of segregation, which affected him both personally and professionally, he spoke out against Little Rock, Arkansas's refusal to integrate its public schools. Armstrong was angered over the white mobs and armed National Guard soldiers who prevented nine African American students from entering the all-white Central High School, despite a federal judge's ruling that the school's population be integrated. Armstrong denounced the governor for calling the National Guard and the federal government for failing to intervene. The events in Little Rock reached a climax just before Armstrong was about to leave on a government-sponsored tour of the Soviet Union. Furious, he canceled the tour, stating, "The way they are treating my people in the South, the government can go to hell." He questioned President Eisenhower's leadership and ended with a heartfelt expression of exasperation, "It's getting so bad, a colored man hasn't got any country." US officials were outraged, but the direct criticism and protest were a sample of what the coming civil rights movement would bring. Some radio stations refused to play Armstrong's records, but he spent most of his time touring, and a year later, the American public had forgotten the controversy. In addition to his protest, 1957 was also the year Armstrong released *Satchmo: A Musical Autobiography* for Decca Records. He renewed his partnership with Ella Fitzgerald when they recorded their second album for Verve.

Over the next two years, Armstrong featured in several films. He appeared in the major motion pictures *The Five Pennies* and *The Beat Generation.* His appearance at the Newport Jazz Festival was recorded in 1958 as well and would appear in the concert film *Jazz on a Summer's Day*, released in 1960. Armstrong also appeared twice on the *Timex Show* on NBC.

In 1959, Armstrong traveled across the pond once more and performed in Sweden, Denmark, the Netherlands, Germany, and Italy. Though he seemed to keep up a superhuman schedule of recordings, performances, and acting gigs, his hectic pace caught up with him while on tour in Spoleto, Italy, where he suffered a heart attack.

Ironically, in the years preceding his heart attack, Armstrong had grown more and more health-conscious. He believed that

Louis Armstrong (*left*), Billie Holiday (*center*), and Barney Bigard (*right*) perform on the set of the musical *New Orleans*.

laxatives were powerful cleansing agents and used them three times a day. He even distributed little packages of his favorite brand to everyone he encountered, including friends, journalists, photographers, and even politicians. He traveled with Joe Glaser's doctor, Dr. Alexander Schiff, who kept an eye on the aging superstar.

On night of June 23, 1959, Armstrong was scheduled to play a show in Spoleto. It was Dr. Schiff who found him on his knees in his hotel room clutching his bedsheets. Schiff called an ambulance, and on the way to the hospital, Armstrong protested, saying, "I don't know why they are taking me to the hospital. I'm fine." He had a fever of 104 degrees Fahrenheit (40 degrees Celsius) when he arrived. An attending hospital worker almost gave Armstrong a dose of penicillin as a remedy, not knowing that Armstrong was allergic to the antibiotic. Luckily, Dr. Schiff was aware of Armstrong's allergy. He lunged across the room and shattered the syringe before the injection could be administered.

News of Armstrong's ill health spread, and Dr. Schiff told anyone who asked that his patient had a case of pneumonia. The Italian doctors went along with the false diagnosis while Armstrong remained in denial about his condition. He couldn't believe his heart could fail him in spite of his regimen. It was indeed a heart attack though, and Armstrong spent the rest of June recovering in the hospital. He went to Rome shortly after being released and rested for a bit before flying to New York and playing unannounced at the city's Lewisohn Stadium on July 4. He only played for fifteen minutes and continued to take things easy until September, when he finally felt well enough to resume his road schedule.

The middle of Armstrong's career began with the trumpet star returning to Chicago with a busted lip, plagued by legal woes and death threats. It took the assistance of Joe Glaser to turn Armstrong's career around. Once Glaser began straightening out Louis's affairs, things got back on track. Both men made a lot of money together, but Glaser was able to spin himself into an entertainment mogul who managed several different black entertainment acts with the Associated Booking Corporation. Armstrong remarried, divorced, and remarried a final time. He was rebranded as Ambassador Satch with relentless foreign tours and worked regularly on tour in the states and in films. His heart attack in 1959 slowed him down, but not for long. He was back doing what he loved, but for how much longer? Only time would tell.

LIFE
VIETNAM
Week of Wild Uncertainty
THE LOUIS ARMSTRONG STORY— AS ONLY HE CAN TELL IT
Salem

9 Satchmo's Legacy

"Musicians don't retire, they stop when there's no more music in them."

Louis Armstrong

Louis Armstrong's heart attack in 1959 was the first serious health concern the jazz giant had faced. However, it would not be his last.

Despite the setback, Armstrong got back to work as soon as possible. By the end of 1959, he had returned to touring in Africa. In the early 1960s, he partnered with fellow jazz icon Duke Ellington. The aging stars both nursed nagging ailments. Louis's lip never completely healed as a result of constant playing, and Ellington suffered from headaches. Nevertheless, the two made some beautiful music together at RCA Studios.

Opposite: Armstrong appeared on the cover of *Life* magazine in April 1966.

The first three years of the 1960s were a whirlwind for Armstrong. In February 1960, he received a star on the Hollywood Walk of Fame. He spent time touring extensively through Africa, filmed the movie *Paris Blues* on location in Paris, recorded with Ellington, and performed at a birthday celebration for President John F. Kennedy in May 1963. As rock 'n' roll began to sweep the globe, Armstrong's jazz was beginning to be associated with a bygone era. However, Louis continued to work and, in fact, was not out of hits. In 1964, he recorded "Hello, Dolly!" The song was a hit and even managed to knock the Beatles out of the number-one spot on the pop charts. His performance of "Hello, Dolly!" won 1964's Male Vocal Performance Grammy, and Armstrong took advantage of the boost in popularity. He toured Puerto Rico and performed in Las Vegas. He also appeared on television as a cohost for *The Mike Douglas Show* and as a mystery guest on *What's My Line?*

Despite Armstrong's health problems at the end of the 1950s, he was on the road again in 1965. He toured Eastern Europe and also returned to New Orleans, where he received the key to the city. He played packed venues in Canada and Las Vegas and continued to appear on television and in films. Armstrong appeared on *The Dean Martin Show* and *Shindig* and filmed the movies *When the Boys Meet the Girls* and *A Man Called Adam.* In April 1966, he was featured on the cover of *Life* magazine. He spent the summer of that year playing the Jones Beach Marine

Theater in Long Island, New York, and appeared on both *The Dean Martin Show* and *The Danny Kaye Show*. The next year he was featured on episodes of *The Tonight Show*, *The Jackie Gleason Show*, and the *Kraft Music Hall Show*. He also performed in *Operation Entertainment*, a concert broadcast from Fort Hood, Texas. Armstrong continued to serve as "Ambassador Satch" and played dates in Ireland, France, and Spain. He also recorded "What A Wonderful World" in 1967, a song that would become forever synonymous with his name.

Armstrong was instrumental in making jazz popular overseas, and his reputation of being America's jazz ambassador was unmatched. Overseas, Armstrong was considered exotic, but he had a dedicated following after several tours of London. Armstrong's international fans followed his career until the end. In February 1968, "What A Wonderful World" was released in the United Kingdom. By April, the song had reached number one on the charts and stayed there for four weeks. The single would not see success in the United States until after Armstrong's death.

While he enjoyed international recognition, Louis Armstrong also continued to captivate American audiences. Also in 1968, Louis continued to tour. He visited several major US cities and played concerts in Mexico. He took some time to film a scene for the film version of *Hello, Dolly!* and recorded *Disney Songs the Satchmo Way*, an album that Walt Disney himself had personally requested two years earlier. Martin Luther King Jr. was assassinated on April 4, 1968. This tragedy affected Armstrong. As a result, he did not attend the Academy Awards ceremony six days later out of respect for the civil rights icon.

Heart and kidney problems plagued Armstrong, too, and he was unable to perform at all in 1969. In fact, he spent February through April hospitalized at Beth Israel Hospital.

Time continued to shake up Armstrong's life. Shortly after he was discharged from the hospital, Joe Glaser was admitted. On June 6, 1969, Armstrong's trusted manager died after suffering a stroke.

Despite Armstrong's health struggles and his grief over the death of his longtime manager, Armstrong felt well enough to make television appearances in 1970 and did a series of concerts in Las Vegas. He made appearances on *The Dick Cavett Show*, *The David Frost Show*, *The Tonight Show*, *The Mike Douglas Show*, and *The Flip Wilson Show*. On July 4, 1970—just shy of a year before his death—Armstrong did an interview with the *New York Times* and reflected on his life: "I think I had a beautiful life. I didn't wish for anything I couldn't get, and I got pretty near everything I wanted because I worked for it."

That year, the Newport Jazz Festival honored Armstrong's life and career. He was rather frail at the time and had lost quite a bit of weight. He could barely muster enough strength to climb a few small steps on his own. He was the picture of retirement in rehearsals as he bumbled around in shorts and a baseball cap. His doctors told him not to risk blowing his horn, but he did sing.

Armstrong appeared on *The Tonight Show* on February 13, 1970.

It was George Wein, the festival's cofounder, who had the idea for Armstrong to take the stage by simply walking out to stand under a spotlight unannounced. Armstrong didn't like the idea. He wanted to come out and launch right into "When It's Sleepy Time Down South," a song he normally opened performances with. Wein got his way, and Armstrong was received with an electric ovation. He looked polished and chic in a bronze-colored suit. He crooned "Mack the Knife" for an adoring crowd, who also got to see Mahalia Jackson, Dizzy Gillespie, Bobby Hackett, and the Eureka Brass Band honor Armstrong's legacy. The success of the show inspired Armstrong to start touring again, and he began to make plans to get back out on the road.

The next year he continued to make the rounds on television shows. He was featured once again on *The David Frost Show*, *The Dick Cavett Show*, and *The Tonight Show*. He also appeared on *The Pearl Bailey Show* and recorded the classic poem "'Twas the Night Before Christmas" in his home. Armstrong did resume touring and visited London, Washington, DC, and New York. On March 30, 1971, he performed in the Big Apple along with Ella Fitzgerald at the opening of the Waldorf Astoria's Empire Room. Armstrong played there for two weeks in spite of the dire warning his doctor, Gary Zucker, had given him before: "You could drop dead while performing." His heart was weak, and Zucker's concern was real. If he pushed himself too much, Armstrong's heart would give out. Still, Armstrong got through the concerts.

Two days after the engagement ended, however, he was back at Beth Israel, having suffered another heart attack.

The press followed Armstrong's condition, and for a time it looked as though he would rebound and be back to touring, singing on television, and acting in films. Later that year, he had a tracheotomy to relieve stress on his lungs and was finally released to his home in the middle of June.

On July 4, members of the press gathered at Armstrong's home in Queens for an interview. He told them he intended to get back out on the road as soon as possible. It seemed he was serious. He contacted his band the next day to see about scheduling rehearsals. However, his body had other plans. The jazz legend was found dead in his home in the early hours of July 6, 1971. He had died in his bed, asleep.

His body was laid in state at the Seventh Regiment Armory at Park Avenue and 66th Street in Manhattan. Outside, twenty-five thousand people waited to pay their respects. His wife Lucille and ex-wife Lil had a private viewing. Lil placed a white handkerchief in his hand, thinking he looked odd without his trademark.

If anyone had any doubt of Louis Armstrong's influence on society, they had to look no further than the sea of mourners gathered at Corona Congregational Church on July 9. Five hundred people filled the church, while another two thousand waited outside behind police barricades. However, Armstrong's New York funeral was not like the boisterous jazz fanfares he had grown up witnessing in New Orleans. No jazz music was played during the ceremony.

Days later, another funeral for the jazz giant took place in New Orleans, and this one looked a lot more like the funeral parades Armstrong had seen in his youth. The Onward Brass Band marched through the streets, playing a swinging rhythm for their own Little Louis.

Finally, Armstrong was laid to rest at Flushing Cemetery in New York City. His pallbearers were all celebrities. Among them were Johnny Carson, New York City Mayor John Lindsay, Dick Cavett, and Merv Griffin.

Armstrong's life continued to be celebrated in the days and weeks that followed. However, on one particular evening, another tragedy occurred. On August 27, 1971, a televised memorial honoring Armstrong's life and work was broadcast from the Civic Center Plaza in Chicago. His ex-wife Lil Hardin was scheduled to perform, though she had been out of the public eye for some time. When she was cued, Lil took the stage and played "St. Louis Blues," smiling and joyful, until she began to struggle to breathe. She collapsed onstage, having suffered a heart attack. The televised affair rolled on as rescue workers attempted to revive Hardin, but it was too late. The woman who had challenged Armstrong to go out on his own and helped him see his full potential had died.

Armstrong left an estate valued at approximately $530,800. Nearly everything went to his wife Lucille. He bequeathed Clarence and his sister five thousand dollars each. Lucille Wilson continued

Visitors at the Louis Armstrong House Museum learn about Armstrong's career and legacy.

to live in the house in Queens that she had shared with her late husband. She received about seventy-three thousand dollars every year in royalties over the next ten years. She spent her remaining years devoted to preserving Armstrong's legacy and passed away in 1983 while visiting Brandeis University for a fundraiser in honor of her late husband.

In 1977, the house Louis Armstrong had lived in with his wife became a National Historic Landmark, and twenty-six years later, on October 15, 2003, it began operating as a museum. The museum is maintained by the City University of New York's Queens College. It is located on 107th Street in Queens, New York. Concerts and educational programs are offered to visitors. The museum also makes its archives of writings, recordings, and memorabilia available for public research.

The Grammy Hall of Fame was established in 1973 in order to pay tribute to songs that have historical significance and were at least twenty-five years old at the time of induction. Over the years, a number of Armstrong's hits have received this honor. In 1974, "West End Blues," a song recorded with his Hot Five group, was the first Louis Armstrong song to be inducted, followed by "St. Louis Blues" almost twenty years later. Armstrong's most recent song to be honored was "Weather Bird" in 2008. The Rock and Roll Hall of Fame lists "West End Blues" as one of the five hundred songs that shaped rock 'n' roll.

Though Ambassador Satch had passed on, his legacy continued to influence popular American music. In 1987, his recording of "What A Wonderful World" was included in the film *Good Morning, Vietnam.* While the song had been a hit in Australia and the United Kingdom years before, it had gone unnoticed in the United States. With the release of *Good Morning, Vietnam*, the song finally received American recognition, cracking the *Billboard* Top 40.

While Armstrong was certainly appreciated in his lifetime, it took years for his influence on American music to truly reveal itself. Armstrong not only laid the foundation for jazz with his perfected solos, swinging rhythms, and innovative timing, he also paved the way for swing music and a modern genre built upon the solo—rock 'n' roll. Both his playing and his singing revolutionized the American sound. Jazz critic and author of *The Encyclopedia of Jazz* Leonard Feather wrote of Armstrong, "His singing, lacking most of the traditional vocal qualities accepted outside the jazz world, had a rhythmic intensity and guttural charm that induced literally thousands of other vocalists to imitate him." Fellow jazz great Miles Davis paid tribute to Armstrong, saying, "You can't play anything on a horn that Louis hasn't played."

It is nearly impossible to separate Louis Armstrong's influence from the basic tenets of American popular music as well as American culture. Armstrong appeared in over thirty films, guest-starred on television programs, and reached audiences via radio broadcast on a regular basis. He became and remained a celebrity during times of great trial for Americans. Through the Great Depression, World War II, and the civil rights movement, Armstrong kept swinging and knew exactly how to stay relevant as popular culture shifted. Jazz adopted his colorful lexicon, too. More and more people in the decades that followed were referred to as "cats," a term Armstrong coined, and suddenly every musician was working on their "chops." Not only was Armstrong revered by fans, but he was highly respected by his colleagues. Both Duke Ellington and Bing Crosby voiced strong admiration for their friend.

Armstrong's body of work has been honored by a number of organizations. In 1972, the Recording Academy awarded Louis Armstrong a Lifetime Achievement Award alongside fellow New Orleanian Mahalia Jackson. A statue of the **virtuoso** trumpet player was unveiled in Armstrong Park in New Orleans in 1980, and in 1995, the United States Postal Service introduced the Louis Armstrong commemorative stamp. *Life* magazine's 1997 list of "The 100 People Who Made the Millennium" listed Armstrong at number sixty-nine. In 1999, he was featured on Variety's "Top 100 Entertainers of the Twentieth Century," as well as *Time* magazine's "100 Most Influential People of the Twentieth Century." National Public Radio recognized "West End Blues," "St. Louis Blues," and "Hello, Dolly!" as part of the "100 Most Important American Musical Works of the Twentieth Century."

Louis Armstrong's magnanimous personality and virtuoso trumpet playing inspired scores of the world's citizens. In fact, his work often spurred others to make art. For instance, Argentinian writer Julio Cortázar credited a 1952 Louis Armstrong concert as the inspiration for Cronopios, fictional creatures that appear in Cortázar's short stories. In 2001, Patrick Neate's novel *Twelve Bar Blues* featured a fictionalized version of Armstrong and was a winner of that year's Whitbread Book Awards. Terry Teachout, a Louis Armstrong scholar, was moved to write a one-man play called *Satchmo at the Waldorf*, which debuted in 2011 and ran

In 1995, the United States Postal Service honored Louis Armstrong with this commemorative postage stamp.

off-Broadway in 2014. In the 1980 film *Stardust Memories*, Woody Allen's character is transfixed by Armstrong's recording of "Stardust" and falls in love with the wrong woman. Writer Ralph Ellison was also a fan of Armstrong's and had seen him perform in 1929. His 1952 novel *Invisible Man* references Armstrong in the opening pages:

> *Perhaps I like Louis Armstrong because he's made poetry out of being invisible. I think it must be because he's unaware that he is invisible. And my own grasp of invisibility aids me to understand his*

> *music ... Invisibility, let me explain, gives one a slightly different sense of time, you're never quite on the beat. Sometimes you're ahead and sometimes behind. Instead of the swift and imperceptible flowing of time, you are aware of its nodes, those points where time stands still or from which it leaps ahead. And you slip into the breaks and look around. That's what you hear vaguely in Louis's music.*

From public statues to posthumous awards to fictional characters that are rendered in his likeness, Louis Armstrong has left such a mark on music that he continues to inspire fans even today. Though he started out poor in New Orleans, Armstrong was able to rely upon the help of Joe Oliver, the Karnofskys, Peter Davis, and other influences to steer him toward success. Through contentious management disputes, rollercoaster marriages, threats from the mob, and breach-of-contract complaints, Armstrong stayed focused on his singing and playing. With the help of Joe Glaser, he was able to stabilize his career and remained culturally relevant for over six decades. Whether through his inspired playing, gravelly singing, daring protests, or happy-go-lucky approach, Louis Armstrong offers something for everyone to be inspired by.

Chronology

1901	Louis Armstrong is born on August 4, though he claimed to have been born on July 4, 1900
1912	Armstrong is arrested on December 31 for firing a gun in public during New Year's celebrations. He is sentenced to the Colored Waif's Home
1914	Armstrong is released from the Waif's Home on June 16
1914–1917	Joe Oliver becomes Armstrong's mentor. Armstrong works odd jobs and plays gigs to support himself, his sister, and his mother
1918	Armstrong takes Joe Oliver's place in the Kid Ory Band, marries Daisy Parker, and performs with Tuxedo Brass Band
1919–1921	Armstrong joins Fate Marable's band on traveling riverboat excursions during the summers and plays for the Kid Ory Band, Tuxedo Brass Band, and other New Orleans bands in the winter
1922	Armstrong joins Joe Oliver in Chicago
1923	Records as a member of King Oliver's Creole Jazz Band for OKeh, Paramount, Gennett, and Columbia Records

1924 Divorces Daisy Parker and marries Lil Hardin, pianist for King Oliver's Creole Jazz Band. Moves to New York City and plays in Fletcher Henderson's orchestra

1925 Moves back to Chicago in November to play at the Dreamland Café. Records with his Hot Five group

1929 Tommy Rockwell becomes Armstrong's manager. Armstrong moves to New York and appears in Broadway musical *Hot Chocolates* and performs at Connie's Inn

1930 Begins hectic touring pace as he travels across the United States. Plays New Cotton Club in Culver City, California, where he is broadcast nightly. Performs in first film, *Ex-Flame*.

1931 Johnny Collins is Armstrong's manager. Tours the Midwest and South and returns to New Orleans after nine years away. Records "When It's Sleepy Time Down South"

1932 Extends gig at New Cotton Club, films "A Rhapsody in Blue," appears in Betty Boop cartoon, and tours England

1933 Tours the United States as well as Scandinavia, Holland, Britain, and Paris

1935 Returns to the United States. Joe Glaser becomes new manager, plays Connie's Inn once more

1936 Appears in *Pennies from Heaven*, publishes *Swing That Music*, and records album with the same name

1937 Appears in *Artists and Models* and is the first African American to host a national radio program

1938 Tours the South, revisits New Orleans, films *Going Places*, divorces Lil Hardin, marries Alpha Smith

1939 Plays six-month gig at the Cotton Club

1940–1941	Tours United States
1942	Divorces Alpha Smith, marries Lucille Wilson
1943	Louis and Lucille move into house in Queens, New York
1944–1947	Appears in *Atlantic City*, *Pillow to Post*, and *New Orleans*. Stops performing with big band and forms Louis Armstrong and His All Stars.
1948	Plays first international jazz festival and makes television debut on *Toast of the Town*
1949	Serves as King Zulu at Mardi Gras in New Orleans, features on the cover of *Time*, tours Switzerland, Italy, and France
1952	Tours Canada, Hawaii, Germany, Belgium, Switzerland, Scandinavia, Italy, and North Africa
1953	Films *The Glen Miller Story*, tours Japan
1954	Publishes *Satchmo: My Life In New Orleans*, tours Australia, records *Louis Armstrong Plays W.C. Handy* for Columbia Records
1955	Performs in the United States, Sweden, the Netherlands, and Italy. Records "Mack the Knife" and *Satch Plays Fats* for Columbia Records.
1956	Records with Ella Fitzgerald for Verve, appears in *High Society*, performs for one hundred thousand people in Ghana where footage for documentary *Satchmo the Great* is filmed.
1957	Cancels government-sponsored tour of Russia, tours South America and Europe. Records with Ella

Fitzgerald again for Verve as well as *Satchmo: A Musical Autobiography* for Decca Records

1958 Films *The Five Pennies*, appears in *Jazz on a Summer's Day*

1959 Performs overseas in Sweden, Denmark, the Netherlands, Germany, and Italy. Has heart attack in Spoleto, Italy, appears on *The Ed Sullivan Show* and the *Bing Crosby Show*

1961 Records ten songs with Duke Ellington

1963 Performs at birthday celebration for President John F. Kennedy

1964 "Hello, Dolly!" knocks the Beatles from number-one spot on charts. July 2 declared "Louis Armstrong Day" at the World's Fair

1965 Appears on *The Dean Martin Show*, receives key to the city in New Orleans, tours Eastern Europe and Canada, films *When the Boys Meet the Girls* and *A Man Called Adam*

1966 Plays summer gig at Jones Beach Marine Theater in Long Island, appears on *The Dean Martin Show* and on the cover of *Life* magazine

1967 Tours Ireland and France, appears on *The Tonight Show* and *The Jackie Gleason Show*. Records "What A Wonderful World" for ABC Records

1968 "What A Wonderful World" is a hit in England and Australia. Armstrong tours the United States and Mexico, records *Disney Songs the Satchmo Way*, does not attend the Academy Awards after the murder of Martin Luther King Jr., struggles with heart and kidney problems, and is hospitalized

1969 Hospitalized from February to April at Beth Israel Hospital, Joe Glaser dies, records for soundtrack of *On Her Majesty's Secret Service*

1970 Plays two weeks in Las Vegas. The Newport Jazz Festival pays tribute to Louis Armstrong, appears on several television shows

1971 Passes away on July 6, 1971, at home asleep in his bed

Glossary

auspicious Indicating future success.

ballad A slow and sentimental, sometimes narrative, romantic song.

bill To promote.

cadenza A decorative bit of music usually improvised in a rhythmic style. Generally occurs at beginning or end of a song.

codify To arrange into a system, organize.

crooner Someone who sings in a soft, low, sentimental tone.

desolate A state of bleak and dismal emptiness.

entr'acte An interval between two acts of a theatrical performance.

epitomize To serve as a perfect model or example.

Great Depression The economic strain felt throughout the world from the end of 1929 until the end of the 1930s. Initiated in the United States by the stock market crash.

Great Migration The shifting of a large part of the African American population from the Southern United States to Northern and Midwestern cities from 1916 until 1970.

Harlem Renaissance A period of cultural, social, and artistic outpouring of work from black intellectuals and creatives that centered in Harlem, New York, from the end of World War I until the mid 1930s.

honky-tonk A dance hall and bar that usually features country music. **l**

lexicon Vocabulary of a person, language, or branch of knowledge.

livid Furious.

lucrative Very profitable.

pigeonhole To categorize rigidly and to the exclusion of other possibilities.

prohibition A period in the United States where there was a ban on the production, movement, and sale of alcohol, lasting from 1920 until 1933.

repertoire A collection of pieces that are regularly performed.

revue A theatrical production that incorporates skits, songs, and dances.

scat A style of singing where words are replaced by improvised rhythmic sounds, popularized in jazz music.

sideman A supporting musician, often plays accompaniment.

torrid Full of difficulty.

tutelage Instruction, usually by an authority figure.

virtuoso A highly skilled artist.

Further Information

Books

Bogle, Donald. *Bright Boulevards, Bold Dreams the Story of Black Hollywood.* New York: Ballantine, 2006.

Braggs, Rashida K. *Jazz Diasporas: Race, Music, and Migration in Post–World War II Paris.* Oakland, CA: University of California, 2016.

Branley, Edward J. *New Orleans Jazz.* Charleston, SC: Arcadia, 2014.

Brothers, Thomas. *Louis Armstrong: Master of Modernism.* New York: W.W. Norton, 2015.

Conwill, Kinshasha. *Dream a World Anew: The African American Experience and the Shaping of America.* Washington, DC: Smithsonian, 2016.

DeVore, Donald E. *Defying Jim Crow: African American Community Development and the Struggle for Racial Equality in New Orleans, 1900–1960.* Baton Rouge, LA: Louisiana State University, 2015.

Fauser, Annegret. *Sounds of War: Music in the United States during World War II.* New York: Oxford University Press, 2013.

Gridley, Mark C. *Jazz Styles.* Boston, MA: Pearson, 2014. Print.

Jarrett, Michael. *Pressed for All Time: Producing the Great Jazz Albums from Louis Armstrong and Billie Holiday to Miles Davis and Diana Krall.* Chapel Hill, NC: University of North Carolina, 2016.

Stricklin, David. *Louis Armstrong: The Soundtrack of the American Experience.* Lanham, MD: Rowman & Littlefield, 2015.

Wall, Cheryl A. *The Harlem Renaissance: A Very Short Introduction.* New York: Oxford University Press, 2016.

Watts, Lewis, and Eric Porter. *New Orleans Suite: Music and Culture in Transition.* Berkeley, CA: University of California, 2013.

Williams, Ted. *Jazz: The Iconic Images of Ted Williams.* Suffolk, UK: ACC Editions, 2016.

Websites

Internet Movie Database: Louis Armstrong

http://www.imdb.com/name/nm0001918

Visit Louis Armstrong's page in the Internet Movie Database and learn about all of his many film credits, including work as an actor and musician.

Louis Armstrong Educational Foundation

http://www.louisarmstrongfoundation.org

The Louis Armstrong Educational Foundation was started in 1969 as a means of giving back "some of the goodness he received." The foundation is dedicated to fostering music education and therapy.

Louis Armstrong House Museum

http://www.louisarmstronghouse.org

The Louis Armstrong House Museum functions as a historical museum that hosts educational programs and events. Visit their website to learn more about the King of Jazz and his career.

Bibliography

Armstrong, Louis, and Richard Meryman. *Louis Armstrong: A Self Portrait.* N.p.: Eakins, 1971.

Armstrong, Louis, and Thomas David Brothers. *Louis Armstrong in His Own Words: Selected Writings.* Oxford, UK: Oxford University Press, 2010.

Bergreen, Laurence. *Louis Armstrong: An Extravagant Life.* London, UK: HarperCollins, 1998.

Bogle, Donald, and Marc H. Miller. *Louis Armstrong: A Cultural Legacy.* New York: Queens Museum of Art, 1994.

Brothers, Thomas David. *Louis Armstrong: Master of Modernism.* New York: W.W. Norton, 2015.

———. *Louis Armstrong's New Orleans.* New York: W.W. Norton, 2007.

Brower, Steven. *Satchmo: The Wonderful World and Art of Louis Armstrong.* New York: Abrams, 2009.

Cline-Ransome, Lesa, and James Ransome. *Just a Lucky So and So: The Story of Louis Armstrong.* New York: Holiday House, 2016.

Collier, James Lincoln. *Louis Armstrong: An American Success Story.* New York: Collier, 1993.

———. *The Louis Armstrong You Never Knew.* New York: Children's, 2004.

Dickerson, James. *Just for a Thrill: Lil Hardin Armstrong, First Lady of Jazz.* New York: Cooper Square, 2002.

Foley, Colin. *Who Was Louis Armstrong?* New York: Rosen Classroom, 2013.

Giddins, Gary. *Satchmo: The Genius of Louis Armstrong*. New York: Da Capo, 2001.

Jones, Max, and John Chilton. *Louis, the Louis Armstrong Story, 1900–1971*. New York: Da Capo, 1988.

McKissack, Pat, and Fredrick McKissack. *Louis Armstrong: King of Jazz*. Berkeley Heights, NJ: Enslow Elementary, 2013.

Old, Wendie C. *The Life of Louis Armstrong: King of Jazz*. Berkeley Heights, NJ: Enslow, 2015.

Panassié, Hugues. *Louis Armstrong*. New York: Da Capo, 1980.

Riccardi, Ricky. *What a Wonderful World: The Magic of Louis Armstrong's Later Years*. New York: Vintage, 2012.

Teachout, Terry. *Pops: A Life of Louis Armstrong*. Waterville, ME: Thorndike, 2010.

Weinstein, Muriel Harris, and Frank Morrison. *Play, Louis, Play!: The True Story of a Boy and His Horn*. New York: Bloomsbury, 2013.

Index

Page numbers in **boldface** are illustrations. Entries in **boldface** are glossary terms.